CAMBRIDGE LIBRARY COLLECTION

Books of enduring scholarly value

History

The books reissued in this series include accounts of historical events and movements by eye-witnesses and contemporaries, as well as landmark studies that assembled significant source materials or developed new historiographical methods. The series includes work in social, political and military history on a wide range of periods and regions, giving modern scholars ready access to influential publications of the past.

Secret Memoirs of Robert, Count de Paradès, on Coming Out of the Bastile

Little is known of the true origins of the French adventurer Victor-Antoine-Claude Robert, Count de Paradès (1752–86). He arrived in Paris in 1778, just as the Franco-American alliance, which guaranteed French military support to the United States against Great Britain, was being signed. Paradès was determined to join the French Army, but lacking the connections to do so, offered his services as a spy. He travelled repeatedly to England, visiting ports and fortifications to gather confidential information. First published in 1791, this work provides a detailed account of Paradès' adventures and misfortune. Written while he was jailed in the Bastille, the book denounces the corruption of ministers who wrongly accused him of state treason after the failure of the 1779 Franco-Spanish 'Armada' against Plymouth. A fascinating historical document, it sheds light on the political relations between France and England during the American War of Independence.

Cambridge University Press has long been a pioneer in the reissuing of out-of-print titles from its own backlist, producing digital reprints of books that are still sought after by scholars and students but could not be reprinted economically using traditional technology. The Cambridge Library Collection extends this activity to a wider range of books which are still of importance to researchers and professionals, either for the source material they contain, or as landmarks in the history of their academic discipline.

Drawing from the world-renowned collections in the Cambridge University Library and other partner libraries, and guided by the advice of experts in each subject area, Cambridge University Press is using state-of-the-art scanning machines in its own Printing House to capture the content of each book selected for inclusion. The files are processed to give a consistently clear, crisp image, and the books finished to the high quality standard for which the Press is recognised around the world. The latest print-on-demand technology ensures that the books will remain available indefinitely, and that orders for single or multiple copies can quickly be supplied.

The Cambridge Library Collection brings back to life books of enduring scholarly value (including out-of-copyright works originally issued by other publishers) across a wide range of disciplines in the humanities and social sciences and in science and technology.

Secret Memoirs of Robert, of Robert, Count de Paradès
on Coming Out of the Bastile

Containing an Account of his Successful Transactions as a Spy in England

Robert de Paradès

CAMBRIDGE
UNIVERSITY PRESS

CAMBRIDGE UNIVERSITY PRESS

Cambridge, New York, Melbourne, Madrid, Cape Town,
Singapore, São Paolo, Delhi, Mexico City

Published in the United States of America by Cambridge University Press, New York

www.cambridge.org
Information on this title: www.cambridge.org/9781108045483

© in this compilation Cambridge University Press 2012

This edition first published 1791
This digitally printed version 2012

ISBN 978-1-108-04548-3 Paperback

SECRET MEMOIRS

OF

ROBERT,

COUNT DE PARADES,

A FRENCH SPY.

———— NON INOPIA HOMINUM, SED DESIDIA, NEGLIGENTIA

ET INSCIENTIA PRÆCIPIENTIUM.   *Tacitus.*

SECRET MEMOIRS

OF

ROBERT,

COUNT DE PARADES,

WRITTEN BY HIMSELF,

ON COMING OUT OF THE BASTILE.

Serving to fupply fome important FACTS for the Hiftory of the
late War;

AND CONTAINING

AN ACCOUNT OF HIS SUCCESSFUL TRANSACTIONS,

AS

A SPY IN ENGLAND,

WITH THE REAL CAUSES OF THE FAILURE OF THE EVER
MEMORABLE EXPEDITION AGAINST PLYMOUTH,

In 1779.

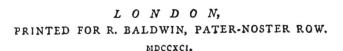

LONDON,
PRINTED FOR R. BALDWIN, PATER-NOSTER ROW.
MDCCXCI.

ADVERTISEMENT

TRANSLATOR.

ALTHOUGH it is not mentioned how the original memoirs were obtained, nor where, nor by whom they were publifhed; yet there are many reafons to believe they contain matters of fact. The plain and unftudied ftyle in which they are written, every where expreffive of the author's emotions, as they arofe at the time, may be confidered as affording an internal evidence of their authenticity. But a ftronger proof may be drawn from the account given of the Combined and Englifh fleets, many of the operations of which are of public notoriety; and with regard to the private tranfactions of the author, fome of them have been confirmed by gentlemen of probity, who perfonally knew the truth of what our author relates on thefe heads. We have, therefore, deemed it a duty to offer a tranfla-

b   tion

tion to the public; for, by bringing to light a part of the fecret correfpondence, which was kept up between this country and France during the laft war, and which narrowly miffed of producing the moft ferious confequences, it was thought it would prove interefting to every Englifhman; and by expofing, as it does, the negligence of fome in office, and the corruption of others, during that period, might render government more watchful on fimilar occafions.

The divifion into chapters, which is adopted in the original, has been difregarded in the tranflation; becaufe it feemed quite unneceffary in a narrative not very long, and no where interrupted; fome minute and tedious details which are by no means effential to the narration, nor interefting to an Englifhman, have likewife been retrenched; and, laftly, care has been taken to leave out many names of men, fhips, and other things, publifhed by the French editors, left they might point out particular perfons as abettors of this enterprifing Spy; and thereby charge them with a criminality,

1   which,

which, notwithftanding the general probability of the author's ftory, ought not to
be done upon fuch evidence.

Some expreffions, which feemed to deferve
the reader's particular notice, have been put
in italics.

ADVER-

ADVERTISEMENT

FRENCH EDITORS.

OUR only motive for publishing these memoirs, of which a great many written copies have gone abroad, is to make the world acquainted with that extraordinary man who is the author of them. We have, therefore, thought proper to suppress the names of many persons therein concerned, as they might, otherwise, have complained of having their secrets divulged.

We have made no alteration in the style of these memoirs. We lay them before the public, just as they were presented to the king. It was in consequence of reading them, that Marshal de Castries, at that time minister of the marine department, interested himself to get Count de Parades released, and to have the remainder of his accounts settled.

Count de Parades died at St. Domingo, in the prime of life.

ADVER-

ADVERTISEMENT

AUTHOR.

NATURE having given me a fpirit of enterprife, attended with great fenfibility, I foon endeavoured to diffipate the obfcurity, that hid, even from myfelf, the authors of my being. I was eager to acquire a name, when I learnt from a refpectable friend that I had one*; and I was anxious to prove by my conduct, that I was worthy of it. Therefore, as foon as I began to reflect, honour and fortune were the only objects of my attention; and I conceived the beft way of acquiring them, was to undertake things evidently hazardous, but which, in cafe of fuccefs, would gain me the rewards I fought. The manner in which I commenced my career had fufficient *eclat* to create envy, and of courfe enemies.

---

* Some fuppofe that M. de Parade's was a defcendant of the family of Parade s in Spain ; others that he was an illegitimate child of a Count de Paradès, a Spanifh grandee, who died in the French fervice ; but moft people are of opinion, that he was only the fon of a paftry-cook at Falfburg.

I have

I have been confined under a fufpicion of having betrayed the interefts of the ftate, when, in truth, I had formed the beft plans for its advantage. My innocence has been proved, and I have been fet at liberty; but as the proceedings againft me were of fuch a nature as not to be publicly known, I now purpofe to lay before government, the manner in which I executed the commiffion that I was charged with by the then minifter; the many opportunities which occurred to me of making my own fortune (all which I was allowed to take advantage of) in the courfe of the whole tranfaction; and, laftly, the fums of money I received from the minifter, and what I paid on the king's account, upon the bufinefs with which I was trufted; and from this ftatement will be feen the propriety of my demands upon his majefty.

It will be perceived, that thefe memoirs are not the work of a lettered man, nor the fruits of much ftudy or reflection. I have reprefented with fimplicity facts relating to myfelf; being perfuaded that truth fhould be the only recommendation of what I have written.

LETTER

LETTER

TO THE

K I N G.

SIRE,

YOU have juſt beſtowed upon
your people the bleſſings of
peace, and added new luſtre to
your reign.   In that war which you
have ſo glorioully terminated, I was
employed to promote the ſucceſs of
your arms, and I was found worthy
of the favours of your Majeſty; but
calumny has made me pay very
dearly for them.   My enemies have
prevailed upon you, by miſrepre-
ſentations, to deprive me of my liberty ; and have ſubjeᶜted to the ſuſpi-
cion of treachery towards you, Sire,

* This letter was written in 1783.

one

one, who, after having exhaufted in your fervice the greateft part of his fortune, would willingly have fhed the laft drop of his blood in the fame caufe.

Thefe memoirs will furnifh your Majefty with an account of my tranfactions and of my difgrace; and there refides in your Majefty's breaft that juftice which is naturally looked for, by

SIRE,

The moft humble,

And the moft refpectful of all

Your faithful fubjects and fervants,

COUNT de PARADES.

A
SHORT ACCOUNT

OF

MY PROCEEDINGS,

From the Firſt of January, 1778, to the Peace in 1782.

AFTER a reſidence of four years in foreign countries, I came to Paris in the beginning of 1778. France was then making thoſe preparations, which indicated an approaching war with England.

I had long had an inclination to enter into the ſervice of government; but it was rather too late for me to engage in that line of life, in the uſual way, as I was 25 years old. I thought that the preſent time might be a favourable opportunity for a more rapid promotion, and I was ſenſible that all my fortune would depend upon my manner of firſt ſetting out.

After having well examined every thing, and conſidered how far my fortune would enable me to

go,

go, I fixed upon the plan of vifiting England, in order to acquire a complete knowledge of that kingdom, of its fea and land forces, of its fortified towns and ports, and thereby to lay the foundation of my future advancement.

Accordingly I put this plan into execution. I repaired to England in the beginning of February; I vifited the principal towns of that kingdom; inquired into, and made memorandums of every thing of importance. Furnifhed with thefe obfervations, I returned to France about the middle of March.

I drew up a fhort account of my journey, which I gave to M. de Sartine, and explained to him, at the fame time, my motives for having undertaken this expedition. The minifter approved of my zeal, promifed me he would give an account of it to the king, and required a few days to look over my papers. When I had the honour to fee him again, he told me he was pleafed with them, but that he wifhed to have a more minute defcription of what they contained. In confequence of this, he charged me to go again into England, to obferve more accurately every port and fortified place, to take exact plans, and draw up defcriptions; to fubjoin feparate ftatements of the Englifh navy, of the number of men of war fitted out, the number

of

of thofe in commiffion, and of thofe upon the ftocks ;
of the dock-yards if poffible, and in general of
every thing that related to the marine department.

I left Verfailles, and came immediately to England. I went over all the places I had feen before, took
an exact lift of all the men of war, frigates, and
other veffels ; I vifited the dock-yards with the moft
fcrupulous attention, and brought back to the minifter a fatisfactory account of every thing concerning which he wanted to be informed.

M. de Sartine expreffed his fatisfaction at the
fuccefs of my journey, and promifed to lay my account of it before the king. I waited upon him
three days afterwards, when he afked me if I thought
it poffible to get faithful agents in the different ports
of England, to give a daily account of what
was going on. I told him I thought it might be
done. He afked me, in the next place, if there
was a poffibility of procuring, on an emergency, an
Englifh veffel for his Majefty's fervice, to watch the
motions of the Englifh fleets, and to convey
immediate intelligence to Breft, or any other place.
I replied that I thought even this was poffible, provided a fufficient fum of money was allowed.

In

In confequence of this, he ordered me to return to England, to make the proper arrangements there, to fecure a correfpondence in cafe of war, and to know what would be the amount of the expences on the firft fetting out, and alfo how much would be afterwards required, in order to keep up the fame eftablifhment. He moreover ordered the fum of 25,000 livres to be paid me immediately, as a reimburfement of the expences which I had incurred in the courfe of the two former journeys.

On my return to England, I imparted to a friend there, fome of the motives which brought me back, and requefted his affiftance. He refufed it, from fear of the bad confequences that might refult from it, to him and his bufinefs ; but he directed me to a perfon who would anfwer my purpofes. With regard to himfelf, he made me promife never to fay any thing more about it, nor to mention his name in any way whatever.

I went to the perfon he had pointed out to me ; and at the third vifit, under pretence of different matters of bufinefs, I brought him at laft to the fubject I wifhed; after which we explained ourfelves more fully, and foon came to an agreement.

He

He engaged to procure me all that I afked, if I would pay him immediately a certain fum of money, and give him, befides, a hundred pounds fterling every month. This being fettled, he recommended me to two Portuguefe Jews, who were let into the fecret, and with whom I left London, to take a third tour, more important, and much more hazardous than the two former.

By the affiftance of my guides, and the letters they had, I formed an acquaintance in every fea port, with fome officer in the marine department, in order to render my correfpondence more general. They all engaged to fend me once or twice a week, an exact journal of what paffed in the port in which they were employed, as well as of the orders they might receive; each making his own terms according as his ambition led him.

It is proper that I fhould here relate what happened to me at Plymouth on this third tour. We got there at midnight, and though I had had no reft for many days, I did not go to bed, that, at the break of day, I might be able to reconnoitre the fort, which I had not fufficiently examined in my former journies.

I took

I took with me a man that I met with upon the key, and got to the fort a quarter of an hour after the gates were open. I paſſed the two firſt ſentinels without interruption ; when I got upon the parade, I turned upon the left, to mount the ſlope which leads to the ramparts. I firſt of all, went over every part of the fortifications which command the country ; I then ſat down upon the ſaliant angle of the baſtion, on the right ſide of the harbour, where I drew the ſketches I wanted. An hour afterwards as I was going to the left baſtion ; and as I paſſed along the curtain (it is neceſſary to notice, that there was not a ſingle ſentinel all round the ram-parts) I was obſerved by the ſentinel before the guard-houſe, who, ſurpriſed at ſeeing two ſtrangers walking upon the rampart ſo early in the morning, went and called out the guard. The ſerjeant came directly to me with two fuzileers. I found it ne-ceſſary to be bold on this occaſion, accord-ingly I went down to meet him as if my walk was over. We met at the bottom of the ſlope. He aſked me, *What buſineſs I had in the fort* ; and ſaid I ought to know that nobody was allowed to come there. I anſwered, that being a ſtranger, I did not know that ; but that the perſon who brought me, ſhould have told me of it, ſince, liv-ing in the town, he ought to have been acquainted with the regulations. *Seize this raſcal,* ſaid the ſer-jeant,

jeant, *and take him to the guard-houſe.* The ſoldiers ſeized my guide by the collar, and carried him
off. I immediately took ten guineas from my
pocket, and offered them to the ſerjeant ; and ſaid,
*Let the poor fellow go, if he has done wrong, it was
certainly without knowing it.* He accepted the money, and ſaid to the ſoldiers, *Turn him out, and don't
let him come in any more* ; then addreſſing himſelf to
me in a milder tone of voice, *Perhaps, Sir, you
wiſh to ſee the fort,* ſaid he, *I am ready to attend you ;
I will juſt go and leave my firelock in the guard-houſe,
and come back in a moment.* As I did not place much
confidence in what he ſaid, I put my papers into
the mouth of one of the cannons, which I pretended to
be examining (there were twelve pieces of ordnance
mounted on the parade). However I need not have
ſuſpected him, for he came back, and went with me ſeveral times round the fort, and took me down to
the batteries which defend the entrance of the harbour, and which are the fineſt I ever ſaw.

I obſerved that the walls before the batteries,
for the ſpace of fourteen yards, were only raiſed
three, four, and five feet high above the rocks upon
which they ſtand ; that theſe rocks, which are very
rugged and broken, ſlope towards the ſea in a de-
clivity of about one foot in every yard ; ſo that it
was a ſhore ſufficiently favourable to land men

upon,

upon, to fcale the walls, and take poffeffion of the
batteries.

I obferved, befides, that the great gate of the
fort, which leads to the batteries, and through
which five men might walk a breaft, was made of
planks only two inches thick, and that it was feldom fhut.

I difcovered under the faliant angle of the left
baftion, a poftern-gate, through which there was
a fubterraneous paffage to the fort (this paffage, as
I afterwards found, is an eafy defcent without fteps).
I took notice, alfo, that the tenaille of the curtain
joined the *revêtement* of the body of the fort; that
it was only twelve feet high, and its platform was
made ufe of for a garden, to which there was a
communication under the curtain, fecured only by
a flight door; that from the tenaille to the top of
the *revêtement*, was only twelve feet, which circumftance made the paffage by thefe fteps a more con-
venient communication, whether that fhould be
thought better than entering by the gates, or whether it fhould be determined to make ufe of both
at the fame time.

The water being lower at the end of my furvey,
I had the fatisfaction to fee that great boats might
land

land at low water, upon a fandy bottom, and that it would be very eafy for men to get up to the batteries, by means of the rocks, which the waves had nearly rubbed into fteps.

After having made all my obfervations, I was fhewn out of the fort, which I had entered at feven in the morning, and did not quit till four in the afternoon. The ferjeant accompanied me to the inn, where I gave him two guineas more for his trouble. On taking leave of me, he protefted he fhould be at my difpofal ever afterwards. I muft remark, that I took my papers out of the cannon, as foon as I perceived that I was in no fort of danger (it will be feen afterwards, how ufeful this man was to me, and how faithfully he ferved me).

I found my two Jews very uneafy about me, and very much alarmed at fo long a ftay. As foon as we had completed the important objeft, which brought us to Plymouth, we went back to London.

My principal agent had not been lefs aftive than myfelf, he had found a captain of a fhip, unemployed, diffatisfied with government, and loaded with debts, who was prevailed upon to enter into my fchemes, in confequence of the emolument he would receive from being appointed commander of the fhip, which the French Minifter wanted to procure.

As

As I was not authorifed to enter into any fixed agreement, I told him, that I could only receive his propofals, which were the following :

" A privateering veffel muft be purchafed, which I will man with 75 failors, or more if neceffary; all the prizes I fhall take from the Americans fhall belong to me, the French government fhall pay me 800 pounds fterling a month, to defray the expences of the crew, and to compenfate me for the rifk I fhall run; the articles agreed upon to continue in force for one year, and a fecurity to be given; a confidential perfon to be put on board my fhip, whofe directions I fhall be bound to follow in all my proceedings; I fhall conform entirely to the orders of the French miniftry; I fhall expect to be paid the fame, whether I happen to be in any of the ports of England, or out at fea; if war fhould be declared between France and England, the terms of the agreement fhall remain the fame, and whatever prizes I take from the French, fhall be divided amongft the fhip's crew; if, contrary to the promife given, I fhould happen to be taken by a French veffel, and fhould be kept a prifoner in France, they fhall be bound to make me amends in the fum of 6000 pounds fterling, to be paid in London; but if I am releafed with my whole crew, they fhall make good to me, in addition to the ftanding agreement, all the loffes I may fuftain."

The

The only difficulty in thefe propofals, was what related to the prizes. I told him that the French Miniftry would never agree to that claufe. He replied, that as he fhould be always guided by their orders, it would be a great chance, if he fhould ever fall in with any of their veffels; but if that fhould happen, he thought he could not avoid taking them; for otherwife, he fhould be obliged to let his crew into the fecret, which would inevitably bring him into very great danger; that, neverthelefs, he would manage matters as well as he could. I did not think proper to infift upon this point any longer, and therefore I prepared to go back to Paris, after having taken an account as near as I could guefs, of the requifite expences for every month; which, including the fhip, the agents in the different ports, the payment of a meffenger from every port to London (as we were afraid to truft to the conveyance by the poft) and from London to Calais, amounted to about 30,000 livres (1250l. fterling).

On my return to Verfailles, I delivered into the hands of M. de Sartine, an exact account of all thefe particulars; he made no objection to the expences, but pofitively refufed to confent to the capturing of veffels. He ordered me to return to London immediately, to conclude the different negociations; and, at the fame time, furnifhed me

with

with 60,000 livres, with a promife of more whenever required.

He moreover ordered me to purchafe a veffel,
and I immediately returned to England, where I
found my captain had met with a fhip of 14 guns,
which was juft come out of dock. I gave 3,500l.
fterling for it, they named it the ————. I afterwards fettled the remainder of the bufinefs on the
the following terms:

	pounds fterl.
To the Captain, for himfelf, his offi- cers, and crew of 75 men or 70 at leaft; including pay, victualling, and other ex- pences, inftead of eight hundred pounds a month, the reduced fum of — —	750
To the principal Agent in London, who had the care of receiving the Meffengers —	100
To the Agent at Portfmouth — —	60
Ditto at Plymouth — — —	60
Ditto at Chatham — — —	40
Salaries for four Meffengers, at fifteen guineas a month each — — —	60
Pofting expences from Plymouth and Portfmouth to London, per month —	50
Four journies a month, from London to Calais — — — — —	25
Hiring of two packet-boats, per month —	12
Renting a houfe in London, my own ex- pences for living, travelling, &c. — —	100

£1257

There

There were befides two Meffengers eftablifhed between Calais and Paris, who were to have 600 livres a year, befides the expences of pofting.

Things being thus fettled, I got a charter-party figned before notaries in London, in which all the former conditions were fpecified, excepting that, inftead of *the orders of the French Miniftry*, my Captain was to proceed according to my directions and thofe of my agents, to any port of Europe or America, to which I fhould chufe to fend him, whether the fhip was loaded with goods or not, &c. I thought this precaution neceffary, as a falvo, in cafe any fufpicion fhould arife, efpecially as this agreement was made before hoftilities were commenced between France and England.

After this, I returned to Paris, without lofs of time, to procure the fum of money I wanted, and to report to the minifter what I had done. He gave me a draft for 7000 pounds fterling, after which I fet out again for London, conformably to his orders, to haften the fitting out of the fhip. On my return, my captain told me, that he was intimately acquainted with a certain perfon who belonged to the miniftry, and if I would let him concert fome plans with him, he would be anfwerable for the fuccefs of
them.

them. I advifed him to make the trial, he did fo, and fucceeded ; and in return for 150 pounds fterling which this perfon afked per month, and which I confented to give, he undertook to fend me a copy of all the orders received at the Admiralty, and alfo of all thofe that fhould be iffued from it. My name was never mentioned in this tranfaction, and I very feldom faw this perfon. To avoid being betrayed, he never put any thing in writing himfelf, but agreed, that the captain fhould wait upon him every day, and read over, and even tranfcribe all the papers, that he fhould lay upon a particular part of his defk ; which was regularly done all the time that I continued in the fervice of France. When my captain was at fea, Mr. ——, formerly governor of——, took upon himfelf the management of this bufinefs, dividing the profits with the captain. He alfo did our bufinefs in London, when we were abfent.

The firft intelligence I received from this perfon was that orders had been fent to Plymouth, for fiting out twelve fhios of the line, which were to fail for America, under the command of Admiral Byron. Thefe orders had been iffued for fome time, but the deftination of this fquadron had been kept fo fecret, that no body knew any thing about it. I received this intelligence forty days before the

fquadron

fquadron fet fail; I immediately difpatched it by a
courier to M. de Sartine, and alfo informed him
how much they were advanced in their preparations,
and which was the day fixed upon for weighing anchor.

The Englifh Miniftry having received information, that twenty-five French men of war had fet
fail from Breft, were apprehenfive that it was with a
defign to attack Byron's fquadron; accordingly orders were difpatched to Admiral Keppel, to leave
Portfmouth with all the fhips he could collect there,
which amounted to twenty; to go in queft of the
French Fleet, watch their motions, and divert their
attention, without however coming to an engagement; and by thefe manœuvres to give Byron's
fquadron an opportunity of getting out of port.
He was farther enjoined, not to lofe fight of the
French fleet, till Byron was fairly out at fea, when he
was to return again to Portfmouth, and continue his
armament. I added to this intelligence, every circumftance that could tend to confirm the truth of
it, namely, that Admiral Byron had taken on board
provifions for feven months, with a large fupply of
mafts and rigging, and his full complement of men;
whilft Admiral Keppel, on the contrary, was to go
out with twenty fhips, of which, the beft equipped
amongft them, would not have fo many as 600 men,

nor

nor provifions for more than twenty days. I could fpeak with certainty refpecting thefe two fquadrons, as I had a lift of every thing that was put on board each fhip.

The whole of this intelligence, was conveyed a fecond time to the French Miniftry, twenty days before the Englifh fleet fet fail; at which time, finding it a good opportunity, I went over to Verfailles. Here I gave an account to M. de Sartine of the new engagements I had made; he approved of them, and even told me, I might promife the perfon a penfion from the king, of 600 livres if he proved faithful*.

After Admiral Keppel had left Portfmouth, in compliance with the orders which he had received, and gone in fearch of the French fleet, he fell in with it at the mouth of the channel; as he was abfolutely forbid to come to an engagement, he took care to keep at a proper diftance from it. The two fleets remained feveral days within fight of each other. The Count d'Orvilliers made no preparations for an attack, being afraid of having thirty-two inftead of twenty fhips againft him, and being miftruftful of the intelligence I had fent. Whilft

---

* This penfion was paid for a year, but was ftopped at the time I was put in the Baftile.

the

the two fleets were watching each other's motions, Admiral Byron paffed behind the French fleet, and got out to fea; and as foon as he found himfelf out of danger, he difpatched a frigate to inform Admiral Keppel of it; who, therefore, returned to Portf-mouth to complete his armament, bringing in with him two French Frigates (the *Licorne* and the *Pallas*) which were captured in confequence of venturing to reconnoitre him too nearly.

This miftruft was the caufe why one of the two fleets was not beaten, and why Admiral Byron was not prevented from proceeding according to his deftination. This fault was difcovered too late to be re-trieved. It was one of the firft that had been committed during this war, and in its effects it proved to be one of the moft fatal. There was another almoft as bad, viz. the ordering of Count d'Eftaing to fail from Toulon with his twelve fhips; whereas, if he had gone from Breft, he would have got to America a month before the Englifh.

I ftopped only two days at Verfailles, after which I came back to London. I found my fhip quite fitted out, and took the command of her, as I did not chufe to truft it to any body elfe; I failed from the Thames to *Spithead*, where I caft anchor by the fide of the Englifh fquadron.

C   In

In the mean time, the Eaſt India Company having received intelligence, by means of a frigate,
which was diſpatched before them, of the arrival of
their whole fleet; orders were ſent to Admiral
Keppel, to ſail from Portſmouth as faſt as poſſible,
in order to join this fleet, to convoy it into port,
and to avoid coming to action, unleſs abſolutely
neceſſary in its defence. At the ſame time, diſpatches were ſent to the Eaſt India fleet, to warn
it of the danger which threatened it, with directions
to keep out at ſea, till Keppel ſhould join it, and ſecure its coming in.

I conveyed this intelligence to Verſailles and to
Breſt, by ſpeedy meſſengers. It was alſo ſent to
Count D'Orvilliers, by means of veſſels, which were
kept in readineſs for this purpoſe.

Keppel ſet ſail from Portſmouth the 10th of July,
with twenty-five ſhips of the line, and was joined by
three others as he paſſed by Plymouth. I followed
him, and kept ſight of him till the 19th, when I
tacked about to the weſt, to meet with the French
fleet. On the 21ſt, being in the latitude 49 degrees
50 minutes, and about 30 leagues to the weſt of the
Scilly iſlands, I diſcovered the French fleet. As I
could not come up to the admiral, on account of
the ſqually weather, which had done me ſome da-
mage

mage, I gave my papers to one of the frigates. The wind blew fo ftrong from the north-weft, that I could not help being driven upon the Englifh fleet. The French fleet was in like manner, obliged to quit its ftation; and was driven towards the mouth of the channel where it fell in with Keppel, who made no other manœuvres, but fuch as might enable him to fail near the wind, for the fake of allowing the Eaft India Company's fleet, which the wind had alfo brought near them, to pafs to the leeward; but on the 27th, when the two fleets came very near to each other, Count D'Orvilliers gave the fignal for an attack, which brought on a general engagement, that continued fome part of the day, after which the two fleets feparated *.

On the morning of the 28th, the Eaft India Company's fleet paffed over the place of the engagement, and entered the channel in fight of fome French men of war that had been feparated from the reft, the day before the action. In all probability this fleet would have been taken, if the French fquadron,

* There was a confufion in the French line, owing to a miftake in the fignals; otherwife, in all probability, it would have been a glorious day for us, as Count D'Orvilliers manœuvres were very judicious.

or

or even a part of it, had kept out at sea twenty-four hours longer*.

I put into Breft after the fleet, to repair the damages I had fustained from the stormy weather. I left that place again on the 2d of Auguft, and came to anchor at Plymouth; where I found a part of the Englifh fquadron had retired.

The feafon being now pretty far advanced, I endeavoured to employ my time *ufefully* in devifing the beft methods for attacking the different ports of England. I began with Plymouth, and drew a very minute plan of it, and of its different harbours and roads, which I founded carefully. I took down memorandums of the fame, and then directed my attention to an object of more importance. I had a trufty perfon, who gave me an exact acccunt of all that paffed in the port; but this was all the bufinefs I employed him in. I did not think him capable of affifting in any great undertaking, and was afraid

---

* Count D'Orvilliers was of this opinion, but as he was prevailed upon to fuffer fo many of the fhips, one after the other, to go into port in order to refit, he found himfelf at laft almoft entirely alone. He therefore thought it beft to follow them, and accordingly gave up the purfuit of the Eaft India fleet. It is fomewhat remarkable, that two-thirds of thefe fhips might have been refitted at fea in four hours time, as was afterwards proved when they came into harbour.

of

of letting him into the fecret of all my fchemes, left he fhould be terrified at them. I bethought myfelf of the ferjeant of the fort, who had been of fuch fervice to me on my third tour, as a more proper perfon to fecond my views. As I did not know his name, nor any perfon, to whom I might apply for it, none of my people being acquainted with him; I could not fail upon any other method, but to walk backwards and forwards in the fort till I I fhould meet with him; which I did on the third day. I went up and fpoke to him, and he feemed very glad to fee me. I told him, I had a fhip lying in the harbour and begged him to come and pay me a vifit (he had too much reafon to be fatisfied with our firft meeting to neglect a fecond). I gave him the name of the fhip, and we parted. The next morning he came on board; and after I had regaled him well, and had made him a prefent of fix bottles of brandy, which he took away with him, he promifed to come to me again the next day.

I had been equally afraid to truft my Captain with the new fchemes that I meditated, as I did not think him daring enough to co-operate with me; therefore, as I could not talk on this fubject before him, when the ferjeant came to me the next day, I went on fhore with him, under pretence of taking a

C 3   walk

walk. I left the failors to look after the boat and we walked off.

After a fhort introduction, I talked to him about his uncomfortable fituation, and offered to make his fortune, if he would ferve me faithfully. He told me, I had behaved fo handfomely the firft time he faw me, that he had been determined ever afterwards to be at my fervice. I faid, that what I wanted him to do for me, was rather a delicate matter, and he would perhaps be alarmed at it, but that with prudence and good management, the danger might be avoided. He replied, that he was ready to do any thing that would oblige me, and that it would not be his fault if he did not change his fituation for the better. Having now brought him to the point I wanted, I explained myfelf fully to him, and let him know that my plan was to contrive how Plymouth might be thrown into the hands of the French. He faid, he had entertained fome fufpicions of the kind the firft time he faw me, from the manner in which I had paid him, but that he was terrified at the greatnefs of the danger. I did not give him time to reflect; here are fifty guineas for you, faid I, befides what you fhall afterwards have; the fame fum fhall be paid to you every month, and 10,000 guineas if the enterprize fucceeds. He had not a word to fay
againft

againſt ſuch an argument. *I am entirely at your ſer-vice, Sir, and ready to do whatever you bid me; only tell me how I muſt proceed.* Such was his anſwer. I do not want any thing done for the preſent, ſaid I; this is a ſcheme which requires a good deal of thought, before it can be put into execution; it is enough for me, that you are in the fort ready to ſerve on any occaſion. I then aſked him, if he was ac-quainted with the perſon who had the care of the ſignals, and with the gate-keeper; he ſaid he was but little acquainted with the former, but that the latter was his friend. Then ſaid I, ſee and make ſure of him, for we ſhall perhaps ſtand in need of him: get acquainted alſo with the keeper of the ſignals, and give me an account of the whole when I come again. I then told him, I was going away in three days time, and enjoined him ſecrecy; we af-terwards returned on board the ſhip, from whence I ſent him back to Plymouth.

My views did not ſtop here. It was doubtful whether the ſerjeant would be able to bring over the keeper of the ſignals, who might otherwiſe give the alarm. I therefore thought of remedying this incon-venience, by making myſelf maſter of the firſt ſignal of the coaſt, which in that caſe, would be made to an-ſwer as I ſhould direct. I had on board an Italian ſailor, called Thomas, whom I had attached to my

intereſt

intereſt by kind treatment. I had put his fidelity to
the teſt for ſome time paſt. I had often had an inclination to let him into my ſecrets; the preſent occaſion
determined me to do ſo. Thomas, ſaid I, I want to
have at my diſpoſal the keeper of the firſt ſignals on
the coaſt; you muſt leave the ſhip and go to him; I
will furniſh you with money, and you ſhall propoſe
to live with him; if he gives his conſent, you ſhall
make yourſelf well acquainted with the ſignals, in
order that you may be able to ſupply his place, on
emergency. If he be a weak man, and in low circumſtances, you may bring him over; but if otherwiſe, you will eaſily contrive to get him out of the
way, at the time he might do us miſchief. I ſent
him off with theſe directions, and thirty guineas in
his pocket.

When he returned on board two days afterwards,
he told me, that having gone to the ſignal keeper as a
deſerter of a ſhip, and begged him to conceal him in
his houſe, he conſented, upon promiſe of being well
paid; after which he left him under pretence of going
to Plymouth, to change his ſailor's clothes, and buy
ſome others. He added, that as this ſignal keeper was
in poor circumſtances, he thought there would be
no difficulty in bribing him; but that at all events,
I might rely upon him, and that he would get rid
of him whenever I had a mind. This ſtation being

at

at a confiderable diftance, one might remain there twelve days, or a fortnight, without being noticed by any body. Upon telling him that we might eafily contrive to get rid of the fignal-keeper, if he could not be brought to comply, he thought that I meant to have him killed, and therefore he offered himfelf for this fervice. This was very far from being my intention ; my defign being only to have him laid hold of by my people, and carried to France, or to keep him on board my fhip as long as there fhould be occafion; which is what I have done in feveral cafes.

Having fettled thefe matters, and put every thing in a proper train, I weighed anchor, and proceeded for Portfmouth. However, I did not fail directly there, but fpent fome time, firft in reconnoitring and founding the harbours and roads of *Start-point* and *Torbay*, and the anchoring places all along the coaft as far as the *Needles* ; fo that I became thoroughly acquainted with them. I then went and anchored before *Yarmouth*, a fmall town in the *Ifle of Wight*, within the *Needles*. On examining this port, I found that it was only defended by a battery of eight pieces of ordnance upon the fhore, and that there was no garrifon. Even at high water none but fmall veffels could come up, and at low water the fhore is dry to a confiderable

diftance

diftance from the town. I remained at anchor here for two days.

I had often paffed before *Hurft Caftle*, a fortrefs built upon a rock ftanding in the fea, and which confifts of a formidable battery that defends the entrance of the Needles. I had not yet had an opportunity of engaging any body there to affift me in my plans. As there were fome foldiers there, though their number was inconfiderable, I did not think it would be fafe to repeat the fame experiments I had tried at Plymouth; I therefore altered my mode of proceeding, and refolved to deceive both my own people and the garrifon, by making both fubfervient to the execution of a fcheme which I had in my head. It was as follows: I told my captain that as I was fatisfied with his fervices, I would put him and the crew in a way of making a good deal of money; that for this purpofe we muft have a landing place upon the coaft, and get fome people on whom we could depend to co-operate with us. I obferved that Hurft Caftle feemed proper for favouring my plans, and that we muft go there together, in order to try if we could concert the proper meafures. Upon his enquiring what they were, I faid that I had in my poffeffion above fifty cafks of brandy, a quantity of wines, and other

ftores,

stores, which should be put on board my ship, and be brought and deposited there ; I told him that he should have all the profits; that he must see and settle matters with the garrison of the fort, in such a manner that they should be ready to receive, in the night time, all the goods we should bring. The captain, who always listened with delight whenever any prospect of gain was held out to him, came into my plan. We went to the fort, and without much ceremony, made our proposals to an officer of the garrison. He called together some others, and stated to them, that a smuggling vessel (for I had called my ship such) proposed to deposit her cargo in the fort, and to divide the profits with them ; that the goods would never be left longer than four days, which was the time that would be required for sending advice to the merchants, who were to take them away. This was easily settled. It was agreed that they should be paid four guineas in ready money, for every cask of wine or brandy that should be left with them, and so in proportion for other goods. After this point was settled we determined upon the signals by which my vessel should be known. It was farther agreed upon, that I should never come but in the night time, and at high water, when they would be prepared to receive me. I left them, saying it would not be long before they would see me again.

On

On my return to Yarmouth, I weighed anchor and went to Cowes, where I had been told there was a small fortrefs. I found it to be a battery of eight pieces of cannon, planted in the form of a horfe fhoe, with only a woman there, who ferved as a keeper of this fham fortrefs. There were fixty militia-men in the town. Cowes harbour, though fmall, is not a bad one ; it will admit of very large men of war to anchor in, and at the time we were there, they were building a 64 gun fhip. I went from thence to Newport, the capital of the ifland, a fmall unfortified town, about fix miles from the fea ; there were 250 foldiers there, which, together with the two batteries and the fixty militia-men juft mentioned in the town of Cowes, made up the whole force of the ifland.

After having remained two days in this harbour, I went to Spithead, and anchored in the midft of the Englifh fleet, that I might examine Portf-mouth. When I had compleated my plans, I de-termined to go to France, and give an account of what I had done to the minifter*.

* I take no notice of my furvey of Portfmouth, as that would lead me into long and tedious defcriptions ; fuffice it to fay, that this, as well as the other Englifh ports, were examined with the fame care as Plymouth.

I had

I had on board feven large cafks of brandy, and
about twelve of wine, that I had taken in at
Breft, with which I meant to put to the teft
my friends at Hurft Caftle; accordingly I failed
round the ifland, and appeared there again fix days
after I had left it. I made the fignals agreed upon,
and they were anfwered. In the mean time I tacked about to fea, till night came on. About ten
o'clock, a little before high water, I came in and
anchored near the fort, and went afhore in one of
the boats, whilft they loaded the long boat. In
lefs than two hours, twelve cafks were conveyed
into the fort, where I followed with fome of my
men. After drinking a glafs together, we parted.
I repeated this experiment three times afterwards
with the fame fuccefs; and my failors, who entered the fort, always out-numbered the garrifon.

After having thus difpofed matters to infure the
fuccefs of any attempts, we might think of, to fur-
prife the enemy, I fteered for France, landed near
Havre de Grace, and went from thence to Verfailles, having ordered my fhip to go and wait for
me in the Thames. I delivered into M. de Sartine's hands the memorandums I had made of all
my proceedings, and he gave an account of them to
the king, who gracioufly prefented me with a commiffion of captain of horfe, dated the 31ft of Auguft, and

I

alfo

alfo with a penfion of ten thoufand livres, the pa-
tent for which I have by me*.

The minifter approved of all my proceedings,
and provided for the encreafing expences, which
amounted to three hundred pounds fterling per
month. As I had agreed with all my agents for a
whole year, I begged M. de Sartine to fupply me,
at once, with the fum total of the expences; re-
prefenting to him that by that means I fhould be
able to make a good deal of money by different
fpeculations in trade, which would not interfere
with my principal bufinefs, and would ferve to conceal the motives of certain meafures which I was
obliged to tranfact openly. He confented to what
I afked, and accordingly ordered me to be paid the
fum of 14,000 pounds fterling, which was pretty
nearly the balance of the whole expences he had fixed for the year. He afterwards inftructed me
how to proceed with my agents, and mentioned
what he wanted to know of the fecrets of the
cabinet; after which I returned to London,
where I arrived on the 12th of September. My
firft care was to fee how each of my agents went
on. At Plymouth I found the fignal and gate-
keepers in my intereft, and I allotted them twenty-

* I only received this penfion for the firft four months, and no
more of it was paid me ever afterwards.

five

five pounds sterling a month. My man Thomas was appointed to the care of the first signal on the coast; it was left entirely to him, and he gave me a particular description of all the signals. The serjeant assured me that in case of attack, he would take upon him to answer for the great gate, which leads to the batteries, being open, as well as the postern-gate at the angle of the bastion, through which the troops might pass one after the other; that moreover he would nail up all the cannons, as I had hinted to him. I paid each of them what they were to receive, and prepared to go to Bristol, and from thence to Ireland.

Before I set out, I heard that eight merchant vessels, which had been taken from the French, were to be sold by auction, and that a good deal might be got by purchasing them. I directed my principal agent to buy them for me in his name; and I then set out for Bristol and Ireland. I visited the different ports of this kingdom where the transports

They were bought for me at the sum of 2200l. sterling, and were afterwards sent to London, under the care of my sailors. Government, who were at that time in want of ships, purchased them for the sum of 6400l. sterling.

No Englishman could have transacted this business with such success, for he would have been obliged to have had the ships insured, and could not have got a sufficient number of sailors. I gained by this transaction a hundred and five thousand livres.

assembled,

affembled, and I perceived that all of them were equally open to be attacked; I took a particular account of them, and fent it to M. de Sartine. I returned afterwards to London, to fuperintend the different tranfactions. I was taken ill there, and laid up for about a month, probably in confequence of the fatigues I had undergone for a twelvemonth paft. It was in the courfe of this expedition, that I had an opportunity of being of ufe to Mr. ————, a marine officer, in the following manner:

He had been fent over to England on a fecret affair by M. de Sartine. While he was at Ply-mouth, fome people who had known him as a pri-foner during the laft war, recollected him again; and upon his going from thence to another port, they fent people after him to keep an eye upon him. Whilft he was making his obfervations, he perceiv-ed that he was watched, and accordingly with-drew; when he heard them fay, *He is a French fpy, an officer of the marine.* As foon as he came to the inn where he lodged, he went up ftairs into his room, and heard the mob cry out, *He is a fpy, we'll take him and have him hanged.* As the landlord would not fuffer them to come into his houfe to feize him, they were obliged to go to the magiftrates for a war-rant. This took up fome time, and at twelve o'clock at night he was ftill at liberty. About this

hour

hour I got to the inn where the tranfaction happened, and was a little furprifed that they were not gone
to bed. The landlord, who was a friend of
mine, took me afide, and in a few words told me
the whole affair. I went immediately to the harbour, and ordered a veffel that I had there to loofe
anchor, and to get ready for failing. I ordered
them at the fame time to fend the boat on fhore;
and then returned to the inn, and went up ftairs to
the French officer, who was in great anxiety. I
bid him muffle himfelf up in my cloak and follow
me, which he did without hefitation. We made
our way out without being noticed by any body,
on account of the obftruction at the door, from
my carriage, which I had ordered to remain
there on purpofe. I took him on board my fhip,
which was juft on the point of failing. The next
day we got to Calais, where I learnt his name and
his rank. He acknowledged that he was indebted
to me for his life. Two days afterwards I came
back again to the fame port, and found they were
quite puzzled to know how the French officer had
made his efcape. I thought it my duty to fave, at
my own peril, a countryman, whofe diftreffed fituation I knew, and whom I fuppofed to have been
fent on fome fecret bufinefs by the minifter. At
different times, I got fhipped off above 300 French
failors or officers, who had made their efcape from

D   prifon,

prifon, and fupplied them with as much money as they had occafion for, without ever applying to government, or any perfon, for reimburfement.

Upon finding that three hundred fail of merchant fhips had rendezvouzed in the Downs, I informed the minifter of it, adding the place to which they were bound, the courfe they were to fteer, and the numbers of their convoy. I alfo fent him word that if he thought proper, I would fet out two days before the fleet, and convey intelligence to Breft, provided he would have a fquadron there ready to intercept it; which he complied with.

After we had got beyond Portland, there came on fuch a terrible fquall, that the Ruffel, a 74 gun fhip, ran foul of the London of 50, which was fplit in two, and went down inftantly; however, about 45 of the crew were faved. Two frigates, and another veffel, were difmafted, and obliged to put back into Portfmouth. My fhip had her main maft broken, her fails torn away, and was driven out to fea. On the 31ft, when I approached the coaft for the purpofe of fheltering myfelf from the ftormy weather, which ftill continued, we were furprifed by one of the moft dreadful gufts of wind ever known in the memory of man, by which our fhip was driven afhore, and ftruck. Half of
our

our crew perished*; above sixty vessels shared the same fate, in this unfortunate night.

I sent my captain to London, with all the men that were saved. When I got there myself, the first thing I set about, was the purchasing of another ship, which was the ————, mounting ten guns, for which I gave 2500l. sterling. I sent M. de Sartine word of the misfortune which had happened to me, and of the new purchase that I had made. He remitted me 4000l. sterling to make good my losses.

I shall now give a statement of the monies I received from government, during the year 1778, as also of the expences which I had been at, to the 1st of January, 1779; together with the state of my own finances at this period.

---

* The head of our ship struck on the sands, and remained fixed in that situation ; ten sailors were thrown over board by the shock ; twenty-two others, who attempted to save themselves in the boat, were lost in consequence of overloading it. I remained with the rest of the crew, clinging to the fore-part of the ship, till the next day, when some people were able to come to our assistance. The ship was shattered to pieces soon after we quitted it. I lost by this accident 32 men, and about 600l. sterling, which I had on board.

A general

A general recapitulation of the sums of money paid by government, from the month of April, 1778, to the 1st of January, 1779, viz.

French livres.

The first sum of money which I received
from M. de Sartine, and which I have
not mentioned before, amounting to   5000

The second, at the time of my third journey to England, amounting to   —   25,000

The third, amounting to   —   6000

The fourth, viz. 7000l. sterling, or   168,000

The fifth, being the balance of the expences for the whole year, paid at once
by the minister, viz. 14,000l. sterling,
or   —   —   —   336,000

Lastly, the 4000l. sterling, remitted me in
London, for making good the losses I
had suffered by the shipwreck   96,000
_____

Sum total of receipts, 28,750l. sterl. or 690,000
_____

A general

A general recapitulation of the money laid out on the King's account, during the year 1778, to the 1st of January, 1779, viz.

French livres.

Expences incurred during the three journies
in England, including the sums of money advanced to the different agents, at
the time of settling the agreements with
them, travelling expences, &c. all which
were approved at the time by M. de
Sartine, amounting to — 65,000

The sum given for the ——, my first
ship, viz. 3500l. sterling, or — 84,000

The expences amounted, according to our
first calculation, to 1257l. sterling per
month; there was an addition to them
of 300l. sterling the next month, which
raised them to 1557l. sterling; the
whole amounting, at the monthly rate of
37,368 livres, for seven months, beginning from the first of June 1778, to 261,576

Goods, and nearly 600l. sterling, lost on
board the ——, my first ship, at the
time of the shipwreck, amounting in all
to — — — 15,000

Purchase of the ——, my second ship,
viz. 2500l. sterling, or — 60,000

Carried over,   485,576

Brought over,   485,576

Sums paid to the two Calais meſſengers for
  ſeven months wages, at the rate of 600
  livres a year for each, amounting to   1,700

Travelling expences to Verſailles and to
  Breſt, from the 1ſt of June   —   4,000

To two horſes killed and one injured by
  the meſſengers   —   2,000

To ſixty guineas, of which a meſſenger was
  robbed as he was carrying it to pay one
  of the agents   —   —   1,440

Sum total of diſburſements, viz. ⎫
20,571l. 10s. ſterling, or   ⎬   493,716
          ⎭

Which being deducted from the ſum total
  of the money received, viz. 28,750l.
  ſterling, or   —   —   690,000

There remained to me in hand, due to
  the king's account, on the 1ſt of January, 1779, the ſum of 8178l. 10s.
  ſterling, or   —   196,284

Progreſſive ſtatement of my own finances, and of the means which I employed to improve them.

French livres.

By the purchaſe which I made of the ſix ſhips at Plymouth, for the ſum of 2,200l. ſterling, and which were afterwards ſold in the Thames for 6,400l. ſterling, I gained 4,200l. ſterling, or   105,600

I had ſhares in ſix privateers, which were fitted out in the Thames at the ſame time with my firſt ſhip. Each of theſe ſhares coſt me 400l. ſterling, amounting in the whole to 2,400l. ſterling. Two of theſe privateers were taken after they had each made a rich prize; the four others took ſeven prizes, amongſt which were two ſhips belonging to the French Eaſt-India Company. By all theſe prizes, added together, after deducting the original coſt of the ſhares, I gained the ſum of 10,200l. ſterling, or   244,800

I had exchanged 18,000 louis d'ors for the ſame number of guineas, in France; and as the exchange upon each guinea was 26 ſous (13d.) in my favour at London, I gained in the whole 1000l. ſterling, or   —   —   24,000

Carried over,   373,400

Brought over,

I received as conditional premiums of in-
surance (in cafe of capture by the Englifh) upon fix fhips belonging to the
French Eaft-India Company, the fum
of 3000l. fterling, at the rate of 500l.
for each; four of them were taken and
brought into England. I returned the
money which I had received upon the
two others, and there remained a balance in my favour of 2,000l. fterling, or* 48,000
A fhip, called the *Two Sifters*, of 400 tons
burden, valued at 20,000l. fterling,
which was known to have been out at
fea for three months, and fuppofed to
be loft, was offered to be infured
at 60 per cent. I was therefore tempted
to take a concern in it. This bufinefs
dwelt upon my mind the whole night,
and in my dream I thought I faw the
veffel arrive: in the morning, what had
occurred to me in my fleep, tempted me

Carried over, 421,400

They had received in England an account of the names and
value as nearly as could be, of all the French Eaft-India Company's
veffels. It was alfo known that they were near home; all the privateers which hoped to make prizes of them, infured them againft
reprifals, and thofe who took no prizes, received back their premiums.

French livres.

Brought over,   421,400

to take the whole infurance upon myfelf. I received for it 12,000l. fterling.
The fhip came home five days afterwards, fo that in confequence of rifking
the lofs of 192,000 livres. I gained   288,000
I had infured fix months fucceffively, the
——— my firft fhip, valued at 4,000l. fterling at the rate of five per cent. every
month; this infurance coft me 1,200l.
fterling; when my fhip was loft, there
came to me 4,000l. fterling, by which
after deducting what I had paid, I
gained a profit of 2,800l. fterling, or   67,200
As I was informed of the taking of the ifland
of Dominica, before it was known in
London, I had an opportunity of gaining in the funds 2,000l. fterling, or   48,000

Sum total of my profits, made as before
ftated 34,400l. fterling, or   —   825,600

I lent out 250,000 livres on bonds. A fhort
time afterwards, I purchafed a houfe at Paris for
70,000 livres, I fpent about 50,000 livres in fur-
nifhing it, and in buying horfes. Independent of
the money belonging to government, I kept in
hand

hand 18,750l. sterling, or 450,000 livres to make farther speculations, as I had hitherto succeeded so well.

At different times I had given in to M. de Sartine, a statement of the several sums of money I had gained, together with the means which I had made use of to acquire them. He was always so good as to express his approbation.

So great an increase of fortune in so short a time, might not have been believed, if I had not pointed out the manner in which it was made. I may add, that if my only object had been to acquire wealth, I could easily have doubled my fortune in the most *fair* and *justifiable* manner; and that I omitted many opportunities of engaging in very beneficial affairs, lest they should have interfered with the more important concerns, with which I was charged by government : the speculations I did make, were quite accidental, and such as I could undertake without much trouble.

In order to prove what I advance, I shall give a particular account of one occurrence, which held out to me a gain of 600,000 livres (25,000l. sterling). I have now by me all M. de Sartine's letters, which confirm the truth of it, and it will be seen from
what

what confcientious motives I declined to take advantage of it. The ――― a fhip of 600 tons, and 32 guns, had been fent into the Levant by a company of Englifh merchants, to be freighted with filks and other Afiatic commodities. She compleated her lading in the European ports, and had proceeded to Port Mahon, where fhe waited a convoy to England, but in vain, as no Englifh man of war arrived during the five months that fhe remained there. The freighters of the fhip being aware of the great injury they would fuffer from her long delay, and concluding that moft of the goods would be fpoilt by being kept fo long in the fummer time in a warm climate, had recourfe to a fraud, by which they expected to make as much money as if the fhip had really arrived at home, with all her cargo in good condition, viz. they were to infure upon bills of lading amounting to double the value of the cargo, and afterwards to caufe her to be taken by the French in order to conceal their villany.

Accordingly they applied to an infurance company in London, and entered the cargo at the value of 2,000,000 of livres (83,333l. 6s. 8d.) which, together with the premium, that they likewife infured, amounted to 2,500,000 livres. They immediately fent advice to the captain of the fhip, who had himfelf a confiderable fhare in the cargo,

to

to fail from Minorca and to proceed to England, with fecret inftructions to let himfelf be taken. The freighters of the fhip, having received information that two men of war, the —— and the —— were fitting out at Toulon, and that they were to join the fleet at Breft, calculated fo nicely the time for the failing of the ——, that fhe left Port Mahon almoft at the fame time that the two French fhips failed from Toulon, and manœuvered fo well, that fhe was taken before fhe got to the Streights.

In the mean while, a few days after the infurance had been made in London, one of the partners in the infurance-company, got intelligence of the real value of the ——, whofe cargo amounted to only 1,100,000 livres, which added to the value of the fhip, might amount to about 1,200,000 livres (50,000l. fterl.) he was likewife informed of the fcheme to get the veffel taken, and of the orders which had been fent for this purpofe to Minorca; but the matter was without remedy, for if the —— was taken, they could not, in that cafe, profecute the freighters for want of fubftantial proofs againft them.

I had pretty large concerns with this infurance, company, fo that I was well known to them. They therefore applied to me to get them out of the fcrape, and offered in cafe the —— fhould be taken, to

I   give

give me 1,800,000 French livres, provided I would
engage to bring her to them, with every thing on
board untouched. The defign of the infurance-
company, was to revenge themfelves of the fraud,
or at leaft to leffen their loffes. Indeed, if the ——
was taken by the French without the infurers being able to prove for certain, the ftate of the cargo,
as happens in fimilar cafes, they would then be
obliged to pay the freighters 2,500,000 livres
(104,166l. 13s. 4d.) whilft, on the other hand, if
the fhip was brought home, with all its cargo untouched, the freighters in that cafe would have
no claims upon the company, and the infurers in
ftead of paying 2,500,000 livres, would only have
to pay 1,800,000 livres, which would be a faving
to them of 700,000 livres.

In confequence of this, the infurers put into my
hands an exact ftatement of the amount of the
——'s cargo. I accepted the propofal, and we entered into an agreement that, provided I fhould
fucceed in bringing the fhip into England, after fhe
was taken, they fhould pay me the fum above mentioned.

I thought this a matter of fufficient confequence,
for a journey from London to Verfailles; where I
gave an account to M. de Sartine of the bufinefs,
and

and offered in cafe the fhip fhould be taken, to depofite the fum of 1,200,000 livres in payment,
both of the third which belonged to the king, and
of the two thirds to be divided amongft the captors,
provided the minifter would caufe the fhip to be
delivered up to me, to bring her to England. M.
de Sartine had too much confidence in me, to think
that I would deceive him with regard to her real
value; he readily came into my plan, by which I
was likely to gain 600,000 livres without any lofs
to the king, or to the crew of the two fhips that
might take her; he even was at the trouble to inform the captains of the two fhips of my propofals.

About a fortnight afterwards, the minifter received advice that the fhip in queftion was taken by
the ——, and brought into Malaga. He fent me
advice of it, and told me to depofite my money at
the hofpital of Toulon, and that he would afterwards fend an order from the king to get the veffel releafed, together with a paffport to carry her
fafe to England. I had not fo much money in my
poffeffion, but I got enough remitted to me from
London, to complete the fum. In the mean time,
M. de Sartine received an anfwer to the letter he
had fent, ftating that the crew of one of the fhips
accepted my offers, but that thofe of the other refufed them, alledging, that the prize was worth above

two

two millions of French livres. No doubt the captain of the prize ſhip was conſulted about this valuation; it was his intereſt to prevent the ſhip from
being returned to England, becauſe he had a ſhare
in the profits ariſing from the fraud; he therefore
perſuaded the French officers that ſhe was worth
twice as much as I had offered. M. de Sartine
who ſaw the matter in its proper light, was upon
the point' of interpoſing his authority to ſettle the
affair, which he might have done with the more
propriety, as he was entitled in the king's name, to
one-third of the profits ariſing from the capture, and
as the crew of one of the ſhips had agreed to our
firſt valuation for their third, but I foreſaw the diſ-
content which this would infallibly excite amongſt
the crew of the other ſhip, and I was afraid they
would accuſe the miniſter of having injured them
for my advantage. I therefore took the liberty to
tell him of this, and gave up the matter entirely.
However, the crew had no reaſon to be ſatisfied
with their own conduct; for about a month afterwards, when the goods were taken out of the ſhip
in order to be ſold, moſt of them were found to be
ſo ſpoiled, that they did not ſell for 500,000 livres
(20,833l. 6s. 8d.) and that upon credit. Thus
the crew loſt 800,000 livres (33,333l. 6s. 8d.)
ready money; I miſſed the opportunity of gaining
600,000 livres, and the inſurance company in London

don loft all. Laftly, the Minifter in order to put
me in a way of ferving myfelf, whilft I ferved the
king, granted me a very unufual favour, which was
paffports for two Englifh veffels, by means of which
I fhould be enabled to carry on trade without any
rifk. I fhall here fubjoin a copy of the letter dated
Verfailles, the 30th of July 1778, which he did me
the honour to write to me on this fubject.

"I acquaint you, Sir, that his Majefty is difpofed to grant you, according to your requeft, the
paffports for the two Englifh veffels, which may
load at one or more Englifh ports, to go to the
French colonies, or to any of our ports in the Me-
diterranean. As it is neceffary that the paffports
fhould contain the names of the captains and veffels, and the number of men on board, and how
many tons burden, you will be fo good as to fend
me thefe particulars, that I may get the paffports
made out." I have the honour to be &c.

(Signed) DE SARTINE.,

It may eafily be conceived what immenfe advantages I might have derived from fuch an act of
favour if I had chofen to make ufe of it during the
war; but that would have required more attention
than the bufinefs which I had to tranfact for the
king (whom I thought entitled to the preference)
permitted

permitted me to give; and luckily for me, fortune threw in my way readier methods, and such as were adequate to my ambitious views.

At the end of January 1779, I left the Thames with the intention of joining a fleet of merchant-men, which were waiting for a convoy in the Downs; but as they were not yet ready to sail, I went and anchored at Spithead. The whole English fleet were laying there at anchor, in no order. The trial of Admiral Keppel which happened soon afterwards, encreased a kind of desertion of the ships, as the principal officers were upon the court-martial; I got in at night and anchored in the midst of the fleet, without exciting the least suspicion. This circumstance, put into my head a scheme, which I hastened to communicate to the minister; and therefore sailed to France. I proposed to him to fit out two fire ships at Brest, with all expedition, which I would bring into Portsmouth along with my ship as two prizes; that whilst I entered with one of these fire-ships by *Spithead*, the other should pass by the *Needles*, and get in during the night at the turn of the tide; that the fleet should be set on fire at each end at the same time, which would infallibly consume the whole. I added, that the least that could happen to those ships that should not be burnt,

E would

would be their running a-ground; since it being
in the middle of the night, they could only cut
their cables, and then they would be wrecked
before they could unfurl their sails to manage the
ships as the anchorage at Spithead was narrow, and
would not admit of their being either carried out
by the tide, or sailing out in the night without danger.

I engaged to take the direction of one of the fire-
ships; and my captain agreed to take charge of the
other, upon condition that he should be paid 25,000l.
sterling, and have a pension settled upon him by
the king, of 12,000 livres, to be paid in France,
where he was afterwards to live. I moreover proposed to the minister to get another vessel fitted out
with 200 soldiers to land, under convoy of two frigates and a man of war, and take possession at the
same time of the fortress of Hurst-Castle, which
commands the passage of the Needles.

M. de Sartine approved of the scheme, and sent
orders to Brest, for fitting out two large fire-ships.
He ordered me to concert the necessary arrangements for facilitating the taking of Plymouth by
surprise, in case they should be inclined to make
the attempt, at the same time, that they were proceeding against the English fleet. He confirmed
the promises that I had made to my captain, and
some

some officers, who were not to receive their rewards but in case of success.

I returned and embarked near Havre, where my
ship was waiting for me. She had been loaded
with brandy in my absence, according to my directions. I appeared the next day at the entrance
of the *Needles*, and in the evening I unloaded all the
goods I had on board, in the fort, with as little suspicion, and as much ease, as I had done before.

The whole merchant fleet that had rendezvouzed
in the Downs, together with that of the East India
Company, being upon the point of sailing, I sent
intelligence of it to M. de Sartine, who ordered a
squadron to be in readiness at Brest, to intercept it.

In the mean time I was called up to London, by
a very disagreeable occurrence. I had loaded with
goods for Brest, a Spanish vessel of 200 tons burden; I was to freight her for three months at the
rate of a 100l. sterling per month; the captain had
bound himself by the charter-party, to touch at all
the ports that I chose to send him to, in the course of
his voyage from London to Spain, on being paid
three louis-dors a day, for every time he should put
into harbour. I commissioned a banker in London,
upon whom I thought I could rely, to see the cargo

com-

compleated. She was loaded with forty tons of beer, forty tons of copper, and the reft in lead: every ton of copper put on board, coft me 2000 livres; the king paid at Breft about 5000 livres for it; fo that upon the forty tons, I fhould have gained a profit of 120,000 livres (5000l.) It was a good fpeculation, but attended with rifk, fince there then was a prohibition, under a very heavy penalty, againft exporting from England fheet-copper for the purpofe of fheathing fhips, which ftill continues. I was obliged to tell my banker and the Spanifh captain, where the fhip was intended to go. The lading was put on board, whilft I was out upon my laft journey to Paris. On my return to Portfmouth, I received advice from the Admiralty, that the Spanifh captain had told them, that the fhip was freighted for Breft. His objeét in this information was to get the cargo forfeited, and come in for a fhare of it. The perfon at the Admiralty who was in my intereft, fent an ex-prefs to me, to come up to London immediately, in order to avert the danger which threatened me. Very luckily, I loft no time, for if I had ftaid a day longer, I fhould have been too late. I applied to my banker, who had fhipped the goods (he was to go fhares in the profits arifing from the cheat, as I afterwards found) I offered to let the bills of lading go under his name, or to fell him the goods.

He

He preferred this laſt propoſal, upon terms very diſadvantageous to me; but as there was no time to loſe, I complied with every thing he choſe; I loſt 25,000 livres upon the original coſt, and I was beſides forced to pay all the expences of unloading and moving the goods, together with the freight of the veſſel, the ſame as if ſhe had gone her voyage. I loſt by this adventure about 2000 louis dors, inſtead of gaining 6000, which I ſhould have done, if I had not had to deal with a couple of knaves.

A few days after I received another check, which occaſioned me leſs loſs, but more alarm. When I went from Portſmouth to London, I had ordered my captain to go and wait for me at *Margate*, where I was to join him again; he went there, and the day that I arrived, 1 found him upon ſhore, with ſome people belonging to the ſhip, who had come to meet me. It was night and we all ſlept on ſhore. About two o'clock in the morning, I was awakened by the captain, who entered my room, in his ſhirt, with a candle in his hand, and came up to my bed, ſaying to me in a low voice: *Count, we are undone, there is a ſtate-meſſenger in my room, who is juſt arrived, he is writing ſomething, and will apprehend you in a minute. I am arreſted, ſee here are my guards. What,* ſaid I, *we are betrayed then? It muſt*

be

be so, said he: I got out of bed to dress myself, frightened, as was natural in such a situation. *Perhaps, there is a chance of getting out of this scrape,* said the captain, *I know the state-messenger, he is a great friend of the governor's* ———— *Stop a moment, while I go and speak to him.* In two minutes, he came back to tell me, *that it was in my power to save us both, that the messenger demanded a thousaud pounds sterling, that he would then say that he had missed us, and that we were got out to sea, at the time he arrived. A thousand pounds,* said I, *he shall have the money,* and immediately put into his hands two bank notes, of 500l. each; in consequence of which the messenger went away. We immediately dressed ourselves, and, without loss of time, repaired to the ship. Besides this, I was obliged to give a few guineas to the pilot, in order to prevail upon him to weigh anchor, as it was night*. A couple of days afterwards, we anchored in the Downs. I thought it would be best to put out to sea; but my captain

---

* All forts of ships and vessels whatever, are obliged to take up a pilot, when they enter the Thames, or go from London; from the moment he gets on board, he is master, if he has a mind to stop, the captain has it not in his power to force him to go on; he has half a guinea for every foot of water which the vessel draws; if the ship is wrecked, or she suffers any injury, the company of pilots is responsible, which is the reason, why they very seldom fail in the river during the night.

insisted

infifted upon ftaying with the fleet there, affuring me that we had nothing more to fear *.

The fleet of merchant fhips having received orders to depart, I fet fail, and got to the mouth of the channel, twenty-four hours before them. I fell in off Ufhant with a fleet of French merchantmen, coming from St. Domingo, part of which were fteering to Havre and St. Malo, whither they were bound: there came on a dead calm here, which lafted for three days. The force of the current drove down upon me two of thefe fhips, each 500 tons burden. I hailed them, and warned them of the danger they were in, advifing them to tack about and put into Breft. I fpoke to five of them in this manner, one after the other; they anfwered they would follow my advice, and the reft of the fleet fhould do fo alfo. I ftrove as much as I could to get into Breft, during the calm, but I found it impoffible, notwithftanding the lightnefs of my fhip. This was a lucky circumftance for the French vef-

* He was very fure of it, for it was only a trick which he had played to rob me of the money. One of his friends was the pretended ftate-meffenger, as I was informed two months afterwards by a nephew of his, whom he had ufed ill, and who, to be revenged of him, came and told me of the fraud, in which he had borne a part. I never once fpoke to his uncle about it, being afraid, that when he found himfelf detected, he would be induced to play me fome worfe tricks.

fels,

fels, for when the calm was over, inftead of following my advice, they failed for the channel. I was
fo vexed at their bad conduct, that I fired a broad
fide upon each, which forced them to change their
courfe. Two amongft them, of 500 tons bur-
then, that had got farther up the channel than the
reft, ran a-ground in attempting to fave themfelves. I wounded fome of their men, and forced
the others to enter Breft, by the paffage *du Four.*
In paffing before *Berthaume,* I fell in with two
frigates as they were coming out of the *Gullet.* I
threw out the fignal for fpeaking. They laid to,
and faid they were fent out in purfuit of a privateer,
that committed great ravages on their coaft. Upon
telling them that I was the privateer they were in
purfuit of, they caft anchor. After I had brought
my fhip into the harbour, I went to Count d'Orvilliers to inform him of the failing of the Englifh
fleet of merchantmen, of the courfe they were to
fteer, and of the different places of rendezvous. He
fent out a fquadron of fix men of war and feveral
frigates to cruife in the latitude in which the Englifh convoy, were to leave the fleet under their
care.

Information was received about a fortnight afterwards, that whilft the fquadron from Breft, was
cruifing in the latitude above mentioned; the fleet
of

of Englifh merchantmen paffed fo near them at ten
o'clock at night, as to difcover by their lights who
they were; in confequence of which, they crowded
fail and changed their courfe. In the morning, at
the break of day, the French fquadron defcried
three fhips lagging behind, which they took, and
learnt from them that they were a part of a large
fleet of merchantmen, which were only convoyed
by a fingle man of war. If the French fquadron
had got there two hours later in the evening, or the
Englifh fleet two hours fooner, they would probably have been all taken; but no body was to blame
for this.

I fhall now return to what relates to myfelf. I
was on board an Englifh privateer, well armed
and manned with failors, who were determined to
rifk every thing to make a bold ftroke. Five or
fix merchant fhips, were a fine fight to them. It
would have been an eafy matter for me to have
manned three of them, and to have ranfomed the
reft, as the Englifh fleet was fo near that I could
not fail of falling in with it in four hours time.
During the courfe of a week that I continued in the
midft of thefe fhips, I came up to two of them,
fpoke a long time with them, by which they perceived my crew were Englifh. They confeffed
that if I had ordered them to ftrike, they would
have

have done it without making any refiftance. I had
letters of marque, and could therefore have made
prizes of thefe fhips; but I prevailed upon my
crew to let them go, upon promifing each of them
ten pounds fterling, as foon as we fhould get into
Breft. Some of them, however, were not fatisfied
with this, but my captain fhewed great firmnefs on
this occafion, threatening to knock the firft man
on the head who fhould make any difturbance about
it, which made them quiet.

I did not feel comfortable all the time we were
within fight of one another; the captain and the
crew might eafily have changed their mind, and I
am to this day quite at a lofs to know how he could
refift the temptation of taking thefe fhips, which,
upon an average, were worth 500,000 French
livres a piece. He might the more eafily have
done this, as he knew that I fhould not dare to
take any fort of revenge upon him in England,
and that he would have enriched himfelf in this way
without danger; but he was faithful to his engagements, and my apprehenfions were ufelefs.

I had on board my fhip nine French failors,
taken from the *Carnatic*, a veffel belonging to
the French Eaft-India Company, which anchored
by the fide of me in the Thames. Thefe nine failors,

lors, amongſt whom were the maſter and the mate, appeared to me to be courageous people, I therefore told them of my apprehenſions reſpecting the behaviour of the crew, and propoſed to arm them ſecretly, to which they conſented ; and with the help of a dagger, a cutlaſs, and a brace of piſtols, with which they were furniſhed, they would have diſabled a part of my crew from fighting, if they had attempted to mutiny, and the reſt would then have ſubmitted from fear ; but all theſe precautions were unneceſſary, as they all remained in ſubjection.

Immediately after I had anchored in Breſt harbour, the Admiral gave out orders, that no body ſhould come aboard my ſhip. At the ſame time I forbid my people to quit her on any pretence whatever. I ſupplied the crew with as much freſh proviſions as they wanted, for the whole month they continued in the harbour. I moreover divided amongſt them, as a reward for their good behaviour, a gratuity of 800l. ſterling, viz. ten pounds to every ſailor, and the remainder to the officers. Two days after my arrival I ſet out from Breſt to go to Verſailles, in compliance with the orders which I had received from the miniſter. I informed him of every occurrence, and in conſequence of the manner in which he ſpoke of me to the king, his majeſty was pleaſed to grant me a penſion of

6000

6000 livres. I here fubjoin a copy of the letter which the minifter did me the honour to write on this fubject, on the 4th of April, 1779.

" S I R,

" I have laid before the king an account of the fervices you have hitherto rendered to government, and his majefty is pleafed with the ardent and in-defatigable zeal which you have difplayed, and of which he trufts you will continue with unabated ar-dour, to give additional proofs. In order to fur-nifh you with the means for fo doing, and to give you at the fame time a teftimony of his fatisfaction, his majefty has juft granted you a penfion of 6000 livres a year, beginning from the 1ft of January in the prefent year ; which fhall be paid to you, either wholly out of the marine department, or at leaft part of it, and the remainder from the department for foreign affairs. It is with pleafure that I ac-quaint you with this inftance of his majefty's favour, which I am perfuaded will increafe your attach-ment to his fervice.

I have the honour to be, &c.
(Signed)   De Sartine."

My account of the ftate of the different ports and harbours, and the method of attacking them, which I pointed out, having been examined before a
board

board of minifters, it was there determined that if matters were fuch as I had reprefented, it would be for the intereft of the ftate to carry my meafures into execution, and to take advantage of the enemy's negligence; but as I had mentioned feveral extraordinary circumftances which they could not readily credit, they refolved, at the fame time that they accepted my propofal, to appoint an officer on whom they thought they could depend, to go over with me to England, to examine into the truth of what I had related, and to fet me right in any particulars in which I might have been miftaken. The perfon appointed was M. de B——, an engineer in the army, who was in confequence ordered to repair to court.

When this officer came, I went with him to the minifter for the war department, where he was informed of the commiffion on which they wanted to employ him. Prince de Montbarey told him, that if he would confent to go, he fhould be rewarded with the Crofs of St. Louis, be promoted to the rank of Lieutenant Colonel, and have a penfion of 4000 livres (166l. 13s. 4d.) fettled upon him; and he promifed, if we fhould execute our commiffion fatisfactorily, that he would raife me to the rank of colonel, make me a knight of St. Louis, and give me a penfion. He made ufe of thefe expreffions,

expreſſions, " I am authoriſed by the king to promiſe you theſe favours ; ſuch are the intentions of
his majeſty, which I am commanded to make
known to you."

M. de B——required twenty-four hours to con-
ſider upon the dangers of the undertaking, and at
laſt determined to engage in it. The miniſter, after having put into his hands ſome written directions, made him a preſent of 12,000 livres (500l.)
which was immediately paid him ; after which we
ſet out for Breſt. The very day we got there we
embarked in my ſhip, and ſailed without delay.
As M. de B——wiſhed to make his firſt obſervations at Plymouth, we ſteered for this port, and
got there the following day, in company with a veſſel from America, which anchored in the Sound
along with us, by the ſide of the guard-ſhip.

As misfortune would have it, my crew were all
drunk at the time of anchoring, which had like to
have occaſioned ſome very ſerious conſequences.
The guard-ſhip having hailed us to know the name
of the ſhip, and where we came from, my captain,
who was intoxicated, gave an inſolent anſwer. The
captain of the guardſhip was gone to ſleep at the
Dock. The lieutenant, who commanded in his
place, being offended at this anſwer, ordered out

I   his

his long boat, and boarded us with 25 armed men. We were fitting quietly at fupper when he entered the cabin with a part of his men, and in an imperious tone, infifted upon knowing to whom the fhip belonged, and who it was that had given fuch an infolent anfwer.

M. de B—— being quite frightened, ran out upon deck, and hid himfelf amongft the failors. My captain, quite confufed at feeing the fhip boarded in this manner, anfwered imprudently, *it belongs to this gentleman*, pointing to me. Both myfelf and M. de B—— were dreffed like common failors. The lieutenant, furprifed to fee me in fuch a drefs, afked me if it was true that the fhip was mine ; I anfwered *yes*, in French. He was ftill more aftonifhed to fee the captain difconcerted. He faid it was his duty to arreft us, and to take me, as the owner of the fhip, to the Dock.

In croffing the deck, to go down into the long boat, I paffed by M. de B——, fhook him by the hand, and gave him a hundred guineas, which I had in my pocket. I fpoke to two failors, on whom I could depend, to take care of him, and carry him off, if poffible, the next day ; after which I quitted my fhip. About 1 o'clock in the morning, as we were near the Dock, I afked the lieutenant if he
knew

knew Mr. ——*. I know but little of him myfelf, faid he, but the captain of the frigate is intimately acquainted with him. Since that is the
cafe, faid I, we will call upon him. When we got
to the Dock, I was taken to the Navy-office, where
we afked for Mr. ———; they defired me to
walk into the parlour, with my guards, and wait
while he got up. He was rather furprifed to fee
me, but without lofing prefence of mind, he inquired into the reafons of my being arrefted, and
then faid to the officer in a firm tone of voice, you
are to blame for having molefted this gentleman;
you may go back on board your fhip again, and
withdraw the foldiers immediately from the floop †.
He afterwards took me a part, and I told him the
whole affair. He perceived that we were in an
aukward fituation; and left me to write to M. de
Sartine, to acquaint him of the danger which threatened us; I alfo wrote to my principal agent in
London, to put him upon his guard. Thefe difpatches were given to one of my couriers, who
fet out without delay.

Whilft I was engaged in writing, my agent went
for the captain of the frigate, with whom he re-

* A perfon in office, my correfpondent.

† I think it neceffary to mention, that the foldiers who accompanied me, were by at the time.

turned

turned about four o'clock in the morning, and upon
giving him a draft for 1500l. sterling, upon my
banker in London, he went on board his ship, and
withdrew the twenty men, who had been left to
guard the ———, my ship. He had all his re-
collection about him on this occasion, and in order
to prevent any suspicion respecting the agreement we
had just made, he informed my captain, who was
on board the frigate, of the manner in which we
had settled the business, and bid him go immediately and clear our vessel of every thing which could
give rise to suspicion ; in consequence of which, as
soon as he got to her, he threw all the casks of brandy and wine overboard, to prevent people from
discovering where the vessel came from.

About nine o'clock in the morning, I went back
to my ship, and found M. de B—— in the hold,
covered up in his hammock, in which he had hidden himself all the night ; we embraced one another
most cordially.

I ordered them to try and get as many of the
casks as they could out of the water again; several of
them were picked up not damaged amongst the rocks
on the shore ; the rest were staved. They brought
them into Plymouth, together with two bags, containing four hundred pieces of cambrick, and some

F   other

other goods, which, in confequence of giving them
fome money, the cuftom-houfe officers carried up
into the town. M. de B—— and I changed our
drefs, and afterwards went to Plymouth to take poffeffion of an apartment which had been engaged for
us there.

The failors, who had been left on board our fhip,
thinking they had got a fure prize, laid hands upon
every thing they could carry off. I complained of
this treatment, and in order to make it appear that
things were done in the regular train, the lieutenant was fined ten guineas for the damages.

M. de B—— employed himfelf for the three
firft days in reconnoitering the fort, which he examined within fide and without, and afterwards the
different harbours and roads. On the fourth day,
on our return from the Dock, at fix o'clock in the
evening, we found at the door of the houfe where
we lodged, fix foldiers and a coach. This was no
pleafing fight, but we could not avoid going in.
We found in the parlour a perfon in command at
the Dock, to whom our landlord introduced us.
He received us without getting up from his chair.
I thought this a bad omen at firft; but it was only
the effect of an indifpofition, which prevented him
from ftirring. " I have heard, Sir," faid he, " that
" you

" you have been here three days; I am come to
" pay my refpects and offer my fervice to you. I
" thought I fhould have had the honour of feeing
" you at my houfe in the Dock; perhaps the or-
" ders there are not to admit any foreigners, have
" prevented you; but we will fet afide this difficul-
" ty in your cafe, and I hope you will come and fee
" me; I will entertain you in the beft manner I can."
I was fo much furprifed at what he faid, that I was
hardly able to make him an anfwer; I recovered
myfelf however enough to tell him how fenfible I
was of the honour he did me, and that if it had not
been for thofe orders (which however I knew nothing of) I fhould moft certainly have fatisfied the
defire I had of paying my refpects to him, and of
forming an acquaintance with a perfon of fuch great
merit; and that fince he permitted me to have
that honour, I fhould wait upon him the next time
I came. After exchanging many compliments, we
began to talk upon different fubjects. The converfation turned of courfe upon the ftate of the fort;
I afked him if there was a ftrong garrifon, and if
it was well provided with provifions and ammunition. He anfwered all thefe queftions without the
leaft referve. " We have not, faid he, fo many
as three hundred militia-men in the Dock; all our regular foldiers have been taken to America; and the
whole number of workmen in the Docks, employed

in

in building fix fhips of the line, does not amount to
four hundred. With regard to provifions, we fhall
have plenty, as they are making preparations here
for victualling the whole fleet; but we have no
ammunition left us." After a converfation of two
hours, he took leave of me, with many expreffions
of efteem and attachment *.

M. de B——, who had been terribly frightened all
the time this vifit lafted, and who trembled at every
queftion I put, had not entirely got the better of
his fears after the gentleman was gone; but infifted
upon going and fleeping on board my fhip, where
he thought he fhould be fafer. I was obliged to
make ufe of my authority to prevent the boatmen
from taking him there, which was a very lucky
circumftance for him; for if I had fuffered him to go,
it would have been all over with him, and we fhould
have been reduced to the greateft difficulties.

A man of war of 90 guns had come out of the
Docks the day before, to go to America; and lay
at anchor near the fort, waiting for a wind. As

---

* It is now three years ago fince I received this vifit, which I can
only attribute to the manner in which my correfpondent there had
been pleafed to fpeak of me to him, and to the view which he might
thereby have, of fcreening both of us from any fufpicions, to which
the affair refpecting my fhip might have given rife.

the number of her crew was very fmall, fhe fent
out her boats in the night, to prefs men from on
board three other veffels befides mine, which were
in the harbour. They only left on board my fhip
a cabin-boy and the fecretary, who had hidden
himfelf amongft fome cafks. All the failors and
officers were taken and carried on board the man of
war in their fhirts. If M. de B—— had been
amongft them, he would have fhared the fame
fate ; the fright he would have been in, his language, every thing would have betrayed him, and
confequently have expofed us to great danger.

At feven o'clock in the morning we heard of this
new vexation, which it was not an eafy matter to
remedy. After having confidered every method,
I refolved upon the boldeft, viz. to go on board
the man of war, and demand my men back again.
Upon being refufed by the captain, who pleaded
his want of failors, I went to the Dock, and called
upon the officer who had behaved fo politely the
day before. I afked him to interfere in getting my
men back again, which he readily did, fending with
me an officer furnifhed with orders to the captain
of the man of war, who in confequence returned
me all my people, excepting the cook, whom he
had concealed ; he apologized to me as well as he

could,

could, and after he had entertained me, we parted good friends.

So many accidents coming on in this manner, one after the other, alarmed M. de B—— fo much, that he would have quitted fuch a difagreeable place immediately, if he had finifhed his obfervations ; but it took him two days more to compleat them.

There were fourteen French merchant fhips, to be fold by auction, in Plymouth harbour ; I bid for a part of them, and got nine for the fum of 4,600l. fterling; which, as foon as M. de B—— had finifhed his obfervations, I fent to London un- der the care of my failors. They were fold there for 13, 14, and 150ol. fterling a piece. By this fpeculation I gained, after deducting what I gave as a prefent to my men, the fum of 7,000l. fterling, or 168,000 French livres. I alfo purchafed, but on the king's account, the ———, a privateer of 14 guns, compleatly fitted out, for the fum of 1,200l. fterling. I meant fhe fhould replace my fecond fhip, which ftood in need of repairs ; and befides this, it was of confequence to have two veffels ready to execute the great enterprifes which were in agitation.

M. de

M. de B—— being much difordered by the fea, we determined to fend my fhip to Portfmouth, and to travel in poft-chaifes. Before we fet out, we went to fee the French prifoners, amongft every ten men of whom, I gave a guinea to be diftributed; as I had done before in all my former journies. About eight o'clock in the evening, the day before we fet out, they came and told me that fome people out of doors wanted to fpeak to me. I went to them, and found three failors, whom I took to be Englifhmen, who, as foon as they faw me, fell upon their knees. I afked them what they wanted, and who had fent them to me. "We are Frenchmen, faid they, who have deferted from a man of war; we are come to beg you to help us to make our efcape; we were advifed to apply to you by your cook; there are twenty of us, and the reft of our companions are fcattered about in different places, but will come to you in the night; your cook tells us that you have refcued above four hundred of our countrymen, by carrying them, at different times, into France." I had never before found myfelf in fuch a dilemma. Was it a fnare which the captain of the man of war laid for me, to be revenged becaufe I had got my men back again from him; or were they really deferters in diftrefs? The defire of affifting my countrymen in fuch a fituation, got the better both of my own

F 4

and

and of M. de B——'s fears ; for that gentleman feeing every thing in a gloomy point of view, thought he fhould be undone by this good action. I ordered a mafter boatman, who was conftantly with me, to take thefe failors on board my fhip, as well as the others who might come in the night and afk to fpeak with me. Before I fet out, I learnt that feventeen of them were got on board ; they weighed anchor at eight o'clock in the morn- ing, and were reftored to their country. Juft as I was getting into the chaife, one of the three re- maining deferters came up to me. As my fhip had failed, there was only one method of faving him; which was to drefs him as my fervant, and place him behind the carriage. Some time after- wards I carried him fafe to France.

We paffed through *Taviftock*, a fmall town, which was made a place of confinement for French officers upon parole. They had only been allowed to walk to the diftance of half a mile ; but at my requeft, and in confequence of a letter which I wrote to one of the general commiffaries, the per- fon who had the care of the prifoners, extended their walk to three miles. Our journey to Briftol took up two days. After M. de B—— had recon- noitered this place, and I had difpatched fome bu- finefs which required my prefence, we proceeded

for

for London, and arrived there two days afterwards. Without making any-ftay, we fet out again for Portfmouth, where we arrived at ten o'clock at night. M. de B—— employed two days in reconnoitering this fea-port, and the town of Gofport, after which he wifhed to go to the Ifle of Wight, but the fea was fo rough that we could not embark. Being thus difappointed, we went by poft to Southampton, where I hired a fmall floop, the mafter of which was in my intereft, being the fame perfon that conftantly took the goods away from Hurft-Caftle. The fea was ftill very rough when we fet fail, and M. de B—— was fo fick, that I could not get him to go round the ifland by water; he therefore contented himfelf with reconnoitering as far as the entrance of the *Needles*; and after he had examined the fortrefs of Hurft-Caftle, we landed at Yarmouth (in the Ifle of Wight) where he recovered a little from his fea-ficknefs. From thence we travelled poft to the different parts of the ifland, which we wanted to fee. After completing our obfervations, we returned to the floop, which had gone to wait for us at St. Helen's, where a part of the Englifh fquadron lay at anchor, the reft being at Spithead; from thence we proceeded to Portfmouth. We faw the *Victory* fail out of harbour, where fhe had remained ever fince the engagement off Ufhant. As we had nothing more to do in this

port,

port, we went to London. M. de B—— made
some observations along the Thames; after that we
went on board my vessel, which was waiting for us
at Dover; from whence we sailed safely to Calais, and
got to Versailles two days afterwards.

In the tour which I had just made with M. de
B——, I had laid out more than 50,000 French
livres, in extraordinary expences. After he had
given in the papers, containing his observations,
they were compared with mine, and were found to
agree entirely. We were only of a different opinion with respect to some plans of attack.

Conformably to the promises which he had received,
M. de B—— was made a knight of St. Louis,
obtained a lieutenant-colonel's commission, and a
pension of 4000 livres, to be continued to his wife
and children after his death. With regard to myself, I received a colonel's commission in the horse
troops, dated the 3d of June. Had not I also a
right to expect the promised reward of the Cross
of St. Louis? For I had exposed myself to much
greater risks than M. de B——, to whom I had
acted as a guide.

In consequence of M. de B——'s report, government determined to make the necessary arrangements

rangements for attacking, not only Plymouth, but also the Ifle of Wight. M. de Sartine and myfelf had never thought of any thing, but making a fudden invafion, the fuccefs of which, in confequence of the fteps I had taken, notwithftanding all the accidents that might arife, was certain; but when my plan was laid before the minifters, after it had been altered in fome parts, and added to in others, it was at laft entirely thrown afide, though the propofals it contained were plain and eafy, viz. I required 4000 men for Plymouth, and 500 for Hurft Caftle; two men of war, two frigates, and two fireſhips. The men were to embark at Breft, as if for America, and after they had got fairly out of harbour, were to be put under my direction. By means of my fhips, I received advice of all the enemy's motions, and was alfo informed by other means of every thing that paffed in the Englifh cabinet I could go to Plymouth, as fafely as I could go from Breft. They were perfectly fupine in England, and had not the leaft fufpicion of the danger that threatened them: but the French minifters thought the meafures which I pointed out, were too feeble, and wanted to make a great affair of it; which very circumftance was likely to render the fuccefs doubtful.

M. de

M. de B—— and myself, were ordered to lay
before the Count de Vaux, our papers containing
the obfervations and arrangements we had made in
England: after examining the fame, he drew up a
plan for attacking Portfmouth, agreeably to the minifter's intentions; and inftead of 4,500 men, and
2,000,000 of livres, which, with certainty of fuccefs, I required; they brought together an army of
30,000 men, and expended 50,000,000 of livres
(2,083,333l. 6s. 8d.) to no purpofe, as I had been
apprehenfive.

I all along ftrongly folicited the minifter of the
war department, for the Crofs of St. Louis, but
could not obtain it, as I had loft his favour, for
reafons which, out of refpect, I forbear to mention.
I was very much hurt at this refufal, yet did not fuffer it to abate in the leaft my zeal in the king's fervice. M. de Sartine was aware of my vexation,
and afked me why I had not received the Crofs of
St. Louis; I told him I was afraid it would never be
granted me, and mentioned my reafons with all that
confidence, with which his kindnefs had long fince
infpired me; he feemed to feel for me, and expreffed
his fatisfaction at my attachment to him. He told
me that it was not in his power, otherwife he would
give me the *Croix de la Marine* immediately; adding

ing that he could not with propriety apply for it at present to Prince de Montbarey, but would get it for me against the time I should join the fleet. He afterwards directed me to procure some English pilots for the combined fleet, and particularly for the Spanish men of war, the officers of which were very little acquainted with the channel.

I told him that all the money which I had received for the current expences, had been disbursed by the 1st of June; and that I had been obliged to lay out a good deal more for extraordinary purposes, and therefore begged him to furnish me with some cash. He said, as I had some property of my own, he should be glad if I would make use of it, and of my credit, to defray the expences of the commission with which I was charged, till the season was over, when he would reimburse me: I had too much confidence in him, to hesitate a moment about fulfilling his wishes. I put into his hands a general statement of what I had laid out, which exceeded by 116,000 livres, the money I had received as may be seen from the following recapitulation.

General

General recapitulation of monies received.

French livres.

Sums received from the minifter at different times, to the 1ft of January 1779, amounting to 28,750l. fterling, or   690,000

Received at Breft in the courfe of the month of March, by an order from M. de la Porte, upon the royal treafury, 100l. fterling, or   2,400

Sum total of receipts up to the 1ft of July   692,400

General recapitulation of the fums paid on the king's account to the 1ft of July, 1779. viz.

French livres.

According to the firft fettling of the accounts, the expences up to the 1ft of January 1779, amounted to 20,571l. 10s. fterling, or   493,716

For fix months current expences, at the rate of 37,368 livres per month, from the 1ft of January to the 1ft of July, amounting to 9,342l. fterling, or   224,208

1000l. fterling paid to a ftate-meffenger, or   24,000

800l. fterling diftributed amongft the crew of the ———, at Breft, for their good behaviour at the time we fell in with the merchant veffels off Ufhant, or   19,200

French livres.

Extraordinary expences on M. de B——'s
account, viz. 200ol. sterling, or   48,000

Sum total of disbursements to the 1st of
July 1779, viz. 33,713l. 10s. sterling, or   809,124

From which, after deducting the money received from government, viz. 28,850l.
sterling, or   692,400

My disbursements on the king's account,
exceeded my receipts, by 4,863l. 10s.
sterling, or   116,724

Recapitulation of the state of my own finances.

In hand on the 1st of January 1779, the
sum of 18,750l. sterling, or   450,000

By profits arising from purchasing ships at
Plymouth, at two different times, viz.
7000l. sterling, or   168,000

Sum total of money, which I should have
had in hand, on the 1st of July 1779   618,000

From which however, in consequence of
my loss, by the freighting of the Spanish ship, there was a deduction amounting to 2000l. sterling, or   48,000

2

French livres

Besides a deduction also of the sums which
 I had advanced for the king, amounting
 to 4,863l. 10s. sterling, or   116,724

Both of which reduced the sum total of my
 money in hand, on the 1st of July to
 18,886l. 10s. sterling, or .   .   . 453,276

Besides the above, there were other extraordinary
expences, which I had incurred, from being obliged
to increase the salaries of my agents; but, as on the
other hand, I did not let my money lie dead, the
profits which I made in different ways from it, ba-
lanced pretty nearly the expences which are not set
down.

In the mean time, the term of the agreement
made with my captain being expired, M. de Sartine, authorised me to renew it upon the same foot-
ing; which I did on my last journey to London, a
few days afterwards.

Just as the French squadron, under the command of Count d'Orvilliers, were on the point of
sailing from Brest, to join the Spanish fleet, and part
of the French army had repaired to the place where
they were to embark; I represented to the minister, that as the English fleet would probably be

fitted

fitted out in lefs than a month, it would be much better, that Count d'Orvilliers fhould go into the Channel with 32 fhips of the line, and fet about the invafion immediately, than be fent to the coaft of Spain. If they had done fo, England would have been reduced to a very awkward fituation; for fhe had not at that time 15 men of war fit to go out, fo that it would have been an eafy matter for the French forces alone, to execute the whole under-taking*; but government thought proper, for reafons, which it is not my bufinefs to enquire into to arrange matters differently.

At the time of my journey with M. de B——, I had acquainted my captain, and my principal agents in London, with the fecrets of my defigns againft Plymouth, and had gradually excited in them ideas of gain, which made them capable of every thing: they were not much furprifed at the vaftnefs of my plans, and inftead of remonftrances, which I naturally expected, they offered to co-operate with me. I therefore informed them par-ticularly of the meafures I had concerted. The only

---

* The truth of this affertion, was proved by what afterwards happened; for the Englifh fleet did not put out to fea for a month after the failing of the French fquadron; and from that time, till the taking of the Ardent, the former were conftantly reinforced by fhips which joined them, as faft as they were fitted out.

circum

circumstance, which could give us any doubt about
our success, was the garrison of 300 men at Plymouth. The person belonging to the Admiralty,
promised he would get an order signed by the
English minister, for withdrawing the garrison, a
fortnight before our project was to be put into execution; provided we would engage to give him
100,000l. sterling to be disposed of as he thought proper. As this sum was not to be paid till a month
after the success of the enterprise, I promised him all
he asked.

On our return, I communicated to M. de
Sartine the particulars of this new engagement,
which required his signature; but he did not chuse
to put it to a bond for 3,000,000 of livres, in an
affair of this nature. The business was therefore
settled in a different way; viz. it was calculated
that the taking of Plymouth, in consequence of the
advantages the French king would gain by it,
would be equivalent to 60,000,000 (2,500,000l.)
and it was agreed that they should secure to me, as a
reward for my services, the twentieth part of every
thing that should be taken, without any restrictions
whatever with respect to the use of it. In consequence of this, the following warrant from the king,
was made out.

" This

" This day the 5th of June 1779, the king being prefent at Verfailles: in confideration of the
important fervices, which we have received from
Count de Parades, colonel of horfe, and of the inftrudtions which he has furnifhed for facilitating the
execution of the enterprifes, which may be undertaken by his majefty's fleets: his majefty has promifed, and does promife, to the faid Count de Paradés, or the bearers of thefe prefents, in his name,
the twentieth part of every thing, which fhall be
taken from the enemy, according to the inftrudtions
of Count de Paradés, whether the captures fhall
confift of fhips, forts or contributions, &c. and in all
cafes in which his majefty's forces fhall make themfelves mafter of a country or town, which fhall not
afford any contribution, he fhall be recompenfed
proportionably to the importance of the objedt, and
according to his majefty's royal bounty. In wit-
nefs whereof, his majefty has figned, with his own
hand, thefe prefents, and has ordered them to be
fealed and counter-figned by me, one of his majefty's principal fecretaries of ftate, and comptroller of
the finances."

Signed, LOUIS.

Underneath, DE SARTINE.

Sealed with the Royal Seal.

With

With the title which this warrant gave me, together with the perfuafion which I ftill had of the
fuccefs of the operations, I thought I had a fecurity,
not only for the money which I had already advanced, but alfo for that which I was going to advance, and likewife for all the engagements I fhould
enter into, on account of the expedition.

I returned to England, renewed my agreements
there for a year to come, procured fome Englifh
pilots for the combined fleet, and completed the neceffary arrangements for the fuccefs of the different
undertakings. All our agents who were let into
the fecret of the defign upon Plymouth, thought
they had a right to demand an addition to their
falaries; accordingly my captain required 300l.
fterling more a month, for himfelf and his crew;
the perfon belonging to the Admiralty, 150l. the
principal agent at London 100l. the agent at Plymouth 60l. the agent at Portfmouth 30l. the reft
were contented with their former pay. I did not
think proper to difpute about the terms, with people who ferved me fo well, and to whom, confider
ing the nature of the circumftances, I would as
readily have given twice as much, if they had afked
for it. All thefe fums added together, made an
addition of 640l. fterling per month, to which the
minifter made no objection.

A few

A few days after my arrival, M. de Sartine ordered me to prepare for going to Breſt, from whence I
was to proceed to join the fleet, which was expeĉted
to arrive every day. After ſettling my family affairs, I went and received from the miniſter, my
final orders on the evening of the 26th of June, and
left Verſailles the next day. I got to Breſt on the
firſt of July, and there delivered into the hands of
the Marquis de la Prevalaye, the miniſter's letter,
which contained orders for the Glory frigate, commanded by the Chevalier de Bavre, to take me on
board, and carry me to the fleet.

I went on board her on the 2d of July, but ſhe
continued at anchor ſome days longer, to complete
her ſtore of proviſions. We afterwards anchored at
Berthaume, that we might lay more in the way for
joining the fleet. The orders of the Miniſter were,
that ſhe ſhould not go out to ſea, leſt the diſpatches
from Government, with which ſhe was charged,
ſhould fall into the enemy's hands.

Some time after I had gone on board, upon hearing that Prince de Montbarey was come to Breſt, I
went there to communicate to him ſome very inte-
reſting news, which I had received from England.
I ſtaid there two days, and afterwards went on board
again. At the ſame time, I ſent M. de Sartine an

account

account of the intelligence which I had received at
fea, informed him alfo that the Englifh pilots*,
which I had been ordered to procure for the combined fleet, had been waiting off Ufhant, ever fince
the 15th, and added that I did not think it proper
that their fhip fhould come into Breft for obvious
reafons.

After waiting 38 days, we defcried the combined
fleet in the morning of the 7th of Auguft, and therefore failed from Berthaume at 10 o'clock, and joined them at night, to the leeward of Ufhant†; I
went on board the admiral's fhip the fame evening,
to deliver the difpatches with which I was charged
by government. I found Count d'Orvilliers fad and
dejected, owing, in a great meafure to the late de-

* Thefe pilots, to the number of 23, ftood government in about
3,000l. fterling, which on account of the long delay of the fleet,
proved to be an ufelefs expence. Not being able to join the combined fleet, they returned to Plymouth.

† It is difficult to conceive how the fleet came to fall to the leeward of this ifland; according to the report of the officers, they conftantly fteered for the Scilly Iflands, but by a very unlucky concur-
rence of circumftances, they were borne upon the coaft near Breft.
During the whole of their courfe, the wind had blown from the
weft, or fouth weft point, which is the only *plaufible* reafon that
can be given. After they had left Breft, to fail for Spain, they fell
to the leeward of Corronna, contrary to all rules; thefe blunders
were owing to the ignorance of thofe who directed the courfe.

ceafe

ceafe of his fon; he alfo complained of the delays he
had met with on the Spanifh coaft, of the want of
provifions and water, and of the ficknefs which prevailed in the fleet. I returned and flept on board
the Glory frigate, which I quitted the next day, the
8th of Auguft, for the admiral's fhip the *Bretagne*,
agreeably to the minifter's orders.

The fame day I had a private conference with the
admiral, who repeated to me what the officers had
already told me, viz. that on account of the wretched
fituation of their fhips, and of the latenefs of the feafon, they defpaired of being able to do any thing.

Owing to contrary winds and a calm, and in confequence of expecting a fupply of provifions from
Breft, the fleet remained for a week within fight of
land to the leeward of Ufhant*.

As I thought it would be expedient to make an
equal diftribution of provifions and water, I took the
liberty to propofe it; but was anfwered that this
would be contrary to cuftom. Accordingly no fuch
diftribution was made all the time the fleet lay to,
or were becalmed; but they were afterwards obliged

---

* The victualling fhips were ready at Breft, as the minifter had
ordered; but the calm, or fome other reafon which I am unac-
quainted with, prevented them from going out.

to

to have recourfe to it at a time when the fea was very rough, and when they fhould have been other-wife employed.

I reprefented to the admiral that it would be bet-ter to double Ufhant, and wait for the victuallers at the mouth of the channel, as by this means we could eafily intercept a rich fleet of Englifh mer-chantmen, of whofe arrival I had received advice *. But this propofal was adopted too late, in confe-quence of the hourly expectation of the victuallers, and in the end was badly executed.

On the 14th, we at laft quitted fight of land, and fteered for the channel, with a weft fouth weft wind; having previoufly fent word to Breft, for the victuallers to join us at the Lizard-point, where we were going. This day at noon, as we were failing in three divifions to the north north eaft, our van made fignals of having difcovered feveral of the enemy's fhips, amongft which we clearly perceived one of 80 guns, from the Bretagne; accordingly the fignal for purfuit was thrown out to the chafing fhips, and to fome of thofe in the line, and the

---

* This fleet, which was coming from America, entered the chan-nel on the morning of the 13th, convoyed by a few frigatee, and a fingle fhip of the line. If we had doubled Ufhant a day fooner, I am convinced they would have been taken.

whole

whole fleet continued its courfe till night, but fet little fail; the chafing veffels were called back in the evening.

I obferved to the admiral, that the fhips which we had feen, were probably the rear guard, or a divifion of the Englifh fleet, which I knew had orders to keep in this latitude*; and could not help expreffing my furprize that the chafing fhips had been called in, and that the whole fleet had not joined in the purfuit: I was anfwered that they had indeed difcovered fix Englifh men of war, which they might eafily take on their return; but that they were convinced that the greateft part of the Englifh fleet was not at fea, but had put back into port, as foon as they had heard of the approach of the combined fleet. In confirmation of this opinion, they had drawn different plans of Spithead, where they had reprefented the fleet as being placed in the forms of a horfe-fhoe, a fquare, and other pofitions, which fecured them from attack. In confequence of fuch falfe reports, our fleet was induced to give up the purfuit.

* Thefe fhips were in reality the rear guard of the Englifh fquadron, whofe main body was fome leagues to the weft. It is therefore probable that if we had continued to chafe them, with our whole fleet, we fhould have come up to them in three or four hours, as we had the wind in our favour; or at leaft we fhould have fatiffied ourfelves that the enemy was out at fea.

I ftill

I ftill perfifted however to remark that it was much more probable that the Englifh fleet would keep at fea, than remain at Spithead, where they might be bombarded from the ifle of Wight, which, as it was in a defencelefs ftate, we might eafily take poffeffion of. But inftead of attending to my arguments, all the officers, excepting the admiral, were of opinion that it would be better to tack to the eaft, and proceed into the channel for the purpofe of examining the enemy's motions. This meafure however was not long perfifted in, for thofe very officers who had advifed it, defired to leave the channel under different pretences.

This being the cafe, I ftated that as the victuallers, which were the only refource and hopes of our fleet, had been ordered to come to the Lizard-point, without any other inftructions, they would be liable to be taken by the enemy, who were behind us. That even fuppofing they fhould get there fafe, they would not know where to find our fleet; that they might, through miftake, join the Englifh fquadron, if they met it*, and that it was

* Thefe victuallers left Breft the day after we failed, and attempted to come to the Lizard-point, agreeably to orders; but they fell in with the Englifh fleet, which chafed them for 24 hours : luckily however, they got back to Breft, without lofing a fingle veffel; and thought it prudent not to go out again, as they did not know where to meet with our fleet.

therefore

therefore proper to difpatch a frigate to inform them of the courfe we were fteering, and of the danger they would run; unlefs indeed we left fix men of war to wait for, and protect them, and to watch at the fame time the enemy's motions.

I was anfwered that there were not frigates enough to fend off at every moment*, that a fleet at fea fhould never be divided†; and that the fix Englifh men of war which had been feen, would be gone quite off the coaft. This laft obfervation made one of them fufpect that thofe fix fhips had come there for the purpofe of diverting the combined fleet, and drawing it away from the channel into the open fea. This opinion was univerfally received, and from being at firft a mere conjecture, it was afterwards looked upon as a certainty. They wondered it had never occurred to them before, that fuch a ftratagem was poffible; though I was perfuaded that nothing of the kind was intended, for the enemy ran much lefs rifk by watching us, with all their forces united, than with a fingle divifion; which however they would not admit.

---

* No fleet had ever fo many frigates to attend it, for they amounted to 25.

† They had juft admitted the reality of a divifion of the Englifh fleet, and yet immediately afterwards faid that the meafure was impracticable, and contrary to the rules of war.

On

On the 15th, at feven o'clock in the morning, as we were fteering to the North with the wind in the Weft, we difcovered land, and therefore tacked about and fteered into the Channel, in fight of the enemy's coaft, bearing down to the Eaft-North-Eaft.

The admiral began now to inquire for the pilots with which I was to provide the combined fleet; I told him that after they had remained at fea for fix weeks, in fight of Ufhant, they were obliged to put back to Plymouth, from whence they would come and join us whenever fent for. I then put into his hands an exact defcription of this port, which had been *fold* to France, and of which we could take poffeffion without ftriking a blow. In the mean time I propofed to get on board fome of the Englifh fifhermen, who being well acquainted with the coaft, would, on being fufficiently paid, act as pilots to the fleet. As the admiral told me he had very little money about him, I offered him 2000 louis d'ors, which I had taken with me to pay the Englifh pilots. He agreed to make ufe of them if there fhould be occafion, and faid that my plan for taking Plymouth fhould be farther examined when we came nearer that port.

On

On the 16th, having the wind in the North-Eaſt, and ſteering Eaſt South-Eaſt, at noon we came within ſight of the Sound, and anchored at the diſtance of about four leagues from Plymouth. It was now deliberated whether we ſhould proceed any farther, or whether, conſidering the wretched ſituation of the French ſhips, it would not be more prudent to return to Breſt, unleſs we ſhould chance to fall in with the victuallers*. I repreſented to the admiral, that if he returned back at a time when he had it in his power to take Plymouth, he would certainly be cenſured by the Court, who would never believe that the difficulties were ſo great as the officers had ſtated ; that he had drawn upon himſelf the attention of all Europe, and that his country expected great things from him; and that if he gave up the invaſion, and returned to Breſt, he would run the riſk of being ſtript of tne laurels he had gained in the courſe of 60 years ſervice. He anſwered, by complaining, that in ſpite of his

---

* But we had left them behind, without leaving orders where they were to find us. In anſwer to this, it was ſaid, that we might receive ſome ſupply of proviſions from St. Malo or Havre ; but was it likely they ſhould be better acquainted in thoſe ports with the diſtreſſed ſituation of the combined fleet, than at Breſt.

The officers plainly ſhewed, by their whole conduct. that they had perſuaded Count d'Orvilliers to proceed as he had done, leaving the Victuallers behind, expoſed to the enemy, only for the ſake of returning to Breſt, under the pretence of a want of proviſions, and ſo ending the ſeaſon.

remonſtrances

remonftrances to the contrary, he had been com-
pelled to fail from Breft and proceed to Spain, before the fleet had taken in a proper quantity of
provifions; and that on his return; when his ftores
were almoft entirely exhaufted, and his men fick,
inftead of being relieved by the expected fupplies,
he was obliged to proceed into the Channel without being able to act. *Gillard* * and *Du Pavillon* †,
faid he, will inform you more particularly of our
diftreffed fituation. Upon applying to M. de Gillard, he told me that they were really reduced to
diftrefs, by a total want of provifions and water,
and by the lofs of men, which increafed every
day ‡.

* Captain and purfer of the admiral's fhip, who conftantly took
care to make the admiral believe, that the fleet would be ftarved
to death, if they did not put back into harbour.

† A diftinguifhed officer in the fleet, who had great knowledge
of tacticks, and was perfectly acquainted with the management
of fignals.

‡ Some of the fhips had taken on board 25 oxen, 60 fheep, and
fowls of all forts, fome more, fome lefs; all this was in a great
meafure confumed, the tables were not fo plentifully covered, and
confequently we had a powerful motive to return to Breft. Many
reafons may be given for the difeafes which prevail in our fleets;
amongft which may be mentioned the putrid exhalations from the
vaft quantity of live-ftock, which is always taken on board to fupply the luxury of the officers' table. Amongft other nations, on
the contrary, the principal officers live in a more frugal manner,
and

5

However, it afterwards appeared (for the fleet did not-get into harbour till the 14th of September) that the French ships had still provisions enough for a month, whilst the Spanish ships had as much as would serve them for three months. The number of sick might amount to about 3000 at fartheft; and the number of those who had died since they had been out, reckoning 10 men from some ships, 3 and 4 from others, and 7 from the Bretagne, amounted to about 200.

I proposed to the admiral to remedy these distresses, in either of the following ways, viz. First, Provided I was furnished with a sufficient number of ships to enter Plymouth, I engaged in writing, and under the penalty of losing my head, to bring the whole fleet to anchor in the Sound, and to supply them with the necessary provisions; or, Secondly, the fleet might anchor in Torbay, where I engaged in like manner to furnish them in a week's time, with 600,000 livres (25,000l.) worth of provisions, for which I was to advance the money.

The remonstrances and opposition of his council, prevented the admiral from adopting, as he seemed inclined to do, the first of these proposals; he how-

and the lieutenants, midshipmen, &c. mess almost the same as the sailors : of these last, there is generally too great a number on board our ships.

ever

ever refolved upon the feeond, viz. the anchoring in Torbay, though even this met with fome oppofition.

In the morning of the 17th, the wind being in the Eaſt, and as we were ſteering in a line of battle to the South South-Eaſt, in order to clear and get round the Start-point, at ten o'clock we defcried to the leeward, four ſhips lying to, one of which was plainly difcovered to be a ſhip of the line. Our people examined them for fome time, and then agreed they were Spaniſh. I had an excellent telefcope, by means of which I thought I difcovered the Engliſh colours ; but to make myſelf more certain, I went up to the top-gallant maſt, where I confirmed my firſt obfervation. That I might be ſtill more certain, I counted the number of our own fleet, and found there were 22 in the van, and the fame number in the rear. Our line of battle was complete ; and at noon the Bretagne having tacked about to the windward, together with the whole line, I had an opportunity of obferving, that the ſquadron of obfervation, and the chafing ſquadron, were both complete. After I had thoroughly fatisfied myſelf that the ſhips in fight were neither Spaniſh nor French, I came down from the maſt, and communicated my obfervations to the admiral, and upon telling him they were certainly Engliſh,

M. de

M. de Vaugirot (aid major to the fleet) exclaimed,
that it was very odd, after he had declared, and
given his word of honour, that he had difcovered
them to be Spanifh fhips belonging to M. de
Cordova's fquadron, a perfon fhould come and
raife any doubts about it! I excufed myfelf, by
faying, that my telefcope might perhaps have de-
ceived me; and no body repeated the obfervations to contradict him. I may add, as a ftill
farther proof that they were the enemy's fhips,
that, although we had made fignal to crowd fail
ever fince the morning, they ftill continued
to lay to. But nothing could turn them from
their opinion, and not a word more was faid
on the fubject till night.

After we had tacked about at noon, as above
mentioned, we fteered N. N. E. till night,
which brought us back again near the Sound; and
as the wind blew towards it, we might have very
eafily entered; accordingly I recommended this
meafure once more, urging, that Plymouth was
without defence, that the fort was only guarded
by a hundred invalids, and that there were not
any other foldiers either in the town or the neigh-
bourhood: that all the batteries were unfit to be
ufed, that the garrifon of St. Nicholas amounted
only to fifty men, and that the harbour was de-

fended

fended by a single frigate only; so that by one
bold stroke we might take possession of it.
I required 600 men, a bomb-vessel, and a fire-
ship, with which I engaged to take possession of
the fort. The admiral seemed willing to comply with my request, but the officers represented
to him that he had no express order from the
Minister, to entrust me with any such enterprise;
that if I did not succeed, as in all probability I
should not, he ran the risk of being reprimanded
by the Court; that the land soldiers which had
been taken on board refused to proceed*, and,
that the marines were not fit for such an expedition: that it would be first of all necessary to
have the Minister's consent in writing, for which
they would apply by the first frigate that should
be dispatched from the fleet; that moreover, it
was not likely that the fort and harbour were in
such a defenceless state as I wished to make them
believe; that two large encampments had been
discovered upon the coast, one on each side of

---

* There were on board the admiral's ship, some companies of
the Burgundy regiment, the commander of which declared in a po-
sitive manner, that he would not suffer any of his soldiers to land,
and at the hazard of their lives, engage in an expedition for which
they were never designed; he had been sent on board, he said, to guard
the ship, and would not quit her till he got to Brest. I learnt afterwards, that he had been instigated to hold out this language in vin-
dication of their refusal.

the

the Sound*, which was a proof that the enemy were upon their guard; that it was even very poſſible that the Engliſh fleet, which had not yet been met with, had retired into the Sound on our approach; and therefore that it would be firſt of all neceſſary to go and make obſervations.

I replied, that I was certain I was right in every thing I ſaid with regard to the ſtate of the Sound and of the fort, and that I had concerted it ſo that we ſhould be ſeconded by people there, as ſoon as we appeared; that as the orders of the Court were to act offenſively, it was left to the Admiral to determine upon the meaſures that ſhould be taken, and to appoint any officer he choſe to head the expedition, and that the rank of colonel entitled me to ſuch command; that with regard to what they ſaid reſpecting the refuſal of the ſoldiers, I would eaſily remedy that, by taking fifteen of the common ſailors, or even a ſmaller number, out of every French ſhip; that the Spaniſh ſhips would not refuſe to give the ſame aſſiſtance; and that many of the marine officers had told me

---

* There was no real encampment, but merely ſome companies of militia ſcattered along the coaſt; and it would have required at leaſt twenty-four hours before they could have got together, as many as three hundred, either at Plymouth or any where elſe.

they

they fhould be very glad to accompany me*. In fpite of all thefe arguments, the Admiral yielded to the inftances of the officers who wanted previoufly to reconnoitre the place. He told me in private, that my youth, together with the circumftance of being a land-officer, were the reafons why they objected; and that the want of a written order from the Minifter to that purpofe, afforded them a plaufible excufe for oppofing me.

Having thus refolved to reconnoitre the Sound; the *Lougre le Mutin*, commanded by the Chevalier de Roquefeuille was fent on this fervice. At fix o'clock, the fleet had got between Eddyfton-lighthoufe and the coaft, and if we had continued in the fame tack, we fhould have reached the entrance of the Sound in an hour's time, as the wind blew to that quarter; but we were fuddenly ordered to tack about, and fteer to fea during part of the night. At eight o'clock the Couronne paffed the ftern of the Bretagne; but did not hail till ten o'clock in the morning, to inform us, that the *Ardent*, an Englifh man of war of 64 guns, had been taken by fome of our frigates. All were then very much furprifed to find they had been miftaken about the fhips, which they had feen the whole day before.

* Several of thefe officers had written to me, requefting me to give in their names to the Admiral, in order to be employed on my expedition, if it fhould take place.

The

The Ardent, which was commanded by Captain Boteler, had failed from Portfmouth, where she had been juft fitted out. Her crew confifted of about 550 men, of which not more than a hundred were failors; she came out of port with her guns loaded but without any ftock of cartridges, which the Englifh feldom make up till they are at fea. She had been ordered to join the Englifh fleet off the Lizard-point. The day after she failed, she defcried the combined fleet fteering round the Start-point, and taking us for the Englifh, made towards us without any fufpicion; and even manœuvred fo as to fall into our line. The Juno frigate, commanded by M. de Marigny, on feeing the Ardent, made fignals to her, which she did not anfwer; whereupon the Juno threw out the fignal of an enemy's ship to the Couronne, which immediately bore down. At the fame time, the Glory and the Gentille frigates came up. The latter fired a broad fide at her yards, and killed many of the men, who were reefing the fails. The Englifh captain perceiving his miftake, attempted to gain the coaft, but the Juno, by a bold manœuvre, croffed her to prevent this, though she was expofed to all the fire of the Ardent. But this ship being unprepared for action, fired only a fingle gun at a time, without being able to load again; the Couronne now came up

H 3   and

and opening her port-holes, prefented her broad fide; but M. de la Touche-Treville, who had the command of her, with a generofity truly admirable, kept from firing, in order to let the frigates, to which the Ardent was afterwards obliged to ftrike, have the honour of taking her.

On the 16th, two Italian failors, who had been fent in a boat from Plymouth, by the captain of my fhip, which was lying at anchor there with the pilots, had come on board the Bretagne, to enquire why we did not come and take poffeffion of Plymouth, as had been long before agreed upon. On queftioning thefe failors, they declared that there was not a fingle man of war in the Sound, that the Englifh fleet had been cruifing for a week paft between the Start and the Lizard-points, which made people fuppofe the combined fleet was the Englifh, till they were able to count the number of fhips.

The teftimony of thefe men was not fufficient to confirm what I had faid; efpecially as it was contradicted by M. de Roquefeuille, who on his return reported, " that he had gone very far into the Sound, and had difcovered 9 men of war of 80 guns, and 6 frigates, and had come fo near them that they hoifted their flag; and befides

fides thefe which he had diftinctly counted, he
had difcovered the mafts of a greater number behind the fort." Nothing could be more pofi-
tive than this; however, I was fo certain that it
was not the cafe, and fo convinced that my captain and the two failors would not deceive me,
that I did not believe a word he faid. I begged
the Admiral to afk M. de Roquefeuille, in what
pofition they lay at anchor; to which he anfwered
that the large fhips lay by the fide of the walls
of the fort, to the left of the Sound, and that
the frigates were farther out.

This account was fo contradictory to the nature of the place, that no body who knew any
thing about Plymouth, could fuffer himfelf to be
impofed upon by it. For the fort is fituated at
the bottom of the Sound, upon a confiderable ele-
vation which joins to the land. The town of
Plymouth is behind it; to the left of the Sound
is fituated the ifland of St. Nicholas, which is
formidable on account of the rocks and fhallows
about it. The only place in which men of war
can conveniently anchor, is on the right fide of
the Sound, though they may indeed anchor near
the fort, when obliged to it, either in entering, or
coming out of dock. But the miftake did not fo
much confift in placing on the left fide what was,

and

and fhould have been on the right, as in repre-
fenting a number of fhips, where there were none;
befides, how was it poffible to fee any of them behind a fort built upon fuch an eminence?

Thefe remarks which I made, excited fome
doubts, and accordingly a frigate was fent out to
reconnoitre the place a fecond time. When fhe
returned, her report entirely coincided with the
former. I was now quite filenced, and it was fettled beyond difpute, that the Englifh fleet, excepting the divifion which had been feen off the
Lizard-point, was blocked up, and the Magicienne
frigate was difpatched with this intelligence
to government.

I again reminded the Admiral of the depen-
dence I had on the truth of what my agents and
the failors had ftated. I remarked, that it was
not probable that the obfervations which had
been made by two different fhips, could agree
fo exactly, and that it was evident that they had
met and compared notes, that they might not
contradict one another. I plainly told him, that
as to myfelf, I not only fufpected, but was even
convinced that both their reports were falfe;
and as a farther confirmation of this, I afked him
to let me go this very night with the two failors

who

who had come on board, and an officer of the marine, and examine the place by land; with a promife
of returning the next day, either in the boat, or in
my own fhip, which was at anchor in the Sound.
The Admiral would not comply, as he was told
that the officers who had made the obfervations were
very well qualified for the purpofe, and that it would
be an infult to doubt their accuracy. They even
talked of punifhing as fpies, the two failors who, as
they faid, had brought a falfe report, and probably
with the intention of deceiving the combined fleet.

It was known at our Court that the Englifh fleet
was cruifing at the mouth of the Channel; and they
moreover knew that the town and fort of Plymouth
were deferted, and that the invalids, and all the in-
habitants had fled as foon as they had difcovered the
combined fleet. They alfo knew that there was
not a fingle man of war in the harbour, that all the
batteries were unfit for ufe, and that they had no gun-
powder left: what then muft they have thought of
the Admiral upon receiving his difpatches, which
ftated that the enemy's fleet was blocked up; they
muft have fuppofed he was out of his fenfes,—this,
however, was by no means the cafe. It was certainly not his bufinefs to reconnoitre the Sound in his
own fhip, but to truft to the report of the officers of
reputed abilities, to whom he delegated that fervice;
                                                  thefe

thefe officers therefore ought to have been tried for the falfe accounts they gave, and, together with the perfons who recommended them, and oppofed my landing, fhould have received all the blame, inftead of the Admiral. Thus I faw the object, to attain which I had been engaged for 18 months, and which had been attended with great fatigues, un-ceafing cares, and extreme dangers, and upon which the king had expended above 120,000 livres (5000l.) at once irretrievably loft.

On the 18th, M. de Marigny, came on board the Admiral's fhip to give an account of the taking of the Ardent; the Admiral expreffed his furprize that he had not brought with him the captain, and fome of the officers of the fhip, to examine them; he an-fwered, that they had already done fo, and that the Englifh captain had told them, he knew nothing more of the Englifh fleet, except that it was cruifing in this latitude, and that he had met with his prefent misfor-tune from miftaking us for them. On his return to England, this officer was tried by a court-martial, and declared incapable of ferving ever afterwards, for having miftaken a fleet of 65 fhips, for one of 39.

The weather now became ftormy, and continued fo for feveral days, accompanied with thunder, which damaged two of our fhips; in confequence of which the Ardent took the place of one of them

in

in the line. On the 23d the weather cleared up, and was almoſt calm; and we were quite aſtoniſhed to find we were more than 80 leagues to the weſt of the Scilly Iſlands, that is, 120 leagues from Plymouth.

On the 24th, with a good breeze from the North North-Weſt, it would have been eaſy for us to have made up a part of our lee way, but the frigates having deſcried twenty ſhips to the South South-Eaſt, the ſignal was given for a general chaſe, which laſted two hours, when they were diſcovered to be our ſquadron of obſervation. This prepoſterous purſuit, which carried us farther away, was owing to the negligence of thoſe who had been appointed to look out. On the 25th we had a fine breeze. The whole fleet lay to at ſeven o'clock in the morning, with orders for all the principal officers to come on board the Admiral's ſhip, to hold a council. The whole of this day was afterwards employed in making an equal diſtribution of proviſions and water, a buſineſs which was the more difficult, as the ſea was very rough. At ſeven o'clock in the evening, the fleet was ordered to ſail under the fore-top ſail all the night.

On

On the 26th, as we were steering to the East North East, under a brisk breeze from the South South-East, the signal was thrown out at noon of ships to the leeward; half an hour afterwards, the signal was made of having discovered twenty sail, and then of 200. These signals were repeated through the whole fleet, when the admiral hoisted the flag for chasing, and every ship crowded sail in an instant. We continued chasing as fast as possible for nearly five hours; but we could not see any thing, and therefore began to be impatient. At this time, the repeating ships of the van made the signal for giving up the chase. They had been sadly mistaken, for there was neither a fleet, nor yet a single ship. In consequence of this chase, we were drawn considerably out of our course, and it required a long time before we could regain the distance we had lost. On this occasion I could not help observing, that if I was in the Admiral's place, I would hold a court-martial upon the officer who made the first false signals, in order to teach the rest to be more careful in their observations in future: and I called to mind what I had before said respecting the mistake which had been committed in reconnoitring Plymouth; and which was proved to be so by the account they had just collected

5

from a neutral veffel, which ftated fhe had been hailed the day before by the Englifh fleet, about twenty leagues farther to the Weft. Thefe remarks of mine were not at all liked, and only ferved to create me enemies.

On the 27th, 28th, 29th, and 30th, nothing remarkable happened. We moved flowly towards the Channel. On the 31ft at four o'clock in the morning, as we were fteering in three divifions to the Eaft-South-Eaft, with a Weft-North-Weft wind, we difcovered the Englifh fleet at the diftance of about three leagues to the leeward. The fignal was immediately given for forming a line of battle, and crowding fail; together with other fignals preparatory to an engagement. At about feven o'clock, the line of battle was nearly formed ; but many of the officers reprefented to the Admiral, that it would be better to order a general chafe, by which means they might furround the enemy in a few hours; however, as we had begun already to fail forward in a line of battle, he refufed at firft to yield to their advice; though he was afterwards fo much preffed and importuned, that contrary to his own opinion, and to that of M. du Pavillon, he fuffered the fignals for a general chafe to be given; in confequence of which the line was broken, and every fhip chafed with all her fail. At eight o'clock, the admiral perceived

ceived his error, repented of having yielded to the
advice of his officers, and ordered the chafe to be
difcontinued. The fignal was again made to form
the line of battle; this required a confiderable time,
as the quick failors of the rear had out-ftripped thofe
of the van; at ten o'clock, however, the line was
formed.

On the other hand, the enemy had loft no time; but
having formed their line of battle early in the morning, they continued to move forward in that order,
and had got confiderably a head. Our people were at
one time in great fpirits, but they foon ceafed, and
changed into a gloomy filence, in confequence of the
unfteadinefs obferved in our manœuvres. There were
violent debates on this account. M. du Pavillon in-
veighed bitterly againft the advifers, threatened to
throw down the telefcope, and laid his life that, if we
had perfevered according to the firft orders, the
enemy would have been intercepted; and he was certainly right. On the other hand, thofe who had advifed the chafe, maintained that if we had begun
with that, we fhould have furrounded them in two
hours time. The Admiral being quite out of hu-
mour at this converfation, ordered them to have
done with it; and turning to Mr. Hamilton, one
of the captains, hold your tongue, faid he, what
have you to do with it; I am forry I attended to
what

what you, and fome others faid; for, as I have more than once had occafion to find, you know nothing of the matter. Whereupon he ordered, what he fhould have done before, that no perfon fhould be admitted into the council-room, which had become the place of general rendezvous, even for the fteerfmen; the midfhipmen and the *gardes marine* walked backwards and forwards there with their hats on, in prefence of the Admiral, each offering his opinion, without any referve or refpect.

I do not know what are the regulations in other countries; but I know that in England, the commander of the fhip is the only perfon who has a right to go into the council room when he pleafes; all the other officers muft wait till they are fent for; and neither the midfhipmen nor their inferiors, are ever admitted; nobody is fuffered to give his opinion, unlefs afked; the deliberations are fecret, the orders are peremptorily given out, and every perfon is refponfible for their execution. It would be difficult to eftablifh this difcipline in France, where the young people pretend to be the beft informed. The event of this day, however, ought to ferve as an example for ever, and fhew of what confequence it is, that the commander's orders be implicitly obeyed; for which, in cafe they are faulty, he alone is anfwerable.

At

At noon, as we were in fight of the Land's end, we defcried three fhips driven confiderably out of the enemy's line, and were in hopes of taking them. At two o'clock, they were more than three leagues afunder from their line, and almoft oppofite to the head of our line; we could very eafily diftin-guifh them. In the morning the Englifh fleet con-fifted of 39 fhips, at noon we could count only 36. I was one of the firft who noticed thefe three detach-ed fhips, which I continued to watch till night. At two o'clock, and again at three, I pointed them out, in hopes that they would throw out the fignals to fome of the fhips in the head of the line, or to the light fquadron, to bear down upon them; but I was anfwered that they could not yet think of break-ing the line, that M. de Cordova, who was in the rear, would be fure to catch them, and that it was befides, impoffible for them to efcape.

I farther remarked at four o'clock, that thefe fhips were oppofite the rear of our line, that they fuffered themfelves to be feparated on purpofe, and though they had all their fail out, they did not make any way; that their manœuvres plainly fhewed they had an intention to pafs behind us; but our officers faid that was not poffible. Laftly, at five o'clock (the wind had changed to the eaft, and then again to the fouth-eaft) one of thefe three fhips,

which

which had been driven farther than the two others, tacked about, and failed before the wind in a north-east direction, and paffed behind us fo quickly, that fhe was foon out of fight; the weather became cloudy, and the two other fhips inftead of keeping near the wind, took the advantage of the dufk of the evening to get off, by fteering to the South South-Eaft. Not only myfelf, but the whole crew were witneffes to the manœuvres of thefe fhips, which were firft rates. The Admiral was equally informed of their motions; but when he fpoke about them, the officers told him, he might make himfelf eafy, for they could not efcape; which, however, they did completely, owing to our negligence. To make matters worfe, at fix o'clock M. de Cordova gave the fignal of having difcovered a fleet to the leeward; in confequence of which we were ordered to tack about, and to make a general chafe.

If we had continued to purfue the enemy, we fhould have certainly overtaken them, and they would then have had no other refuge but Spithead, where we fhould have blocked them up, which would have been a fine ftroke for us; for we fhould then have been mafters of the fea, and of the Ifle of Wight, from whence they could have eafily been bombarded and deftroyed;

I   but

but all our hopes were gone from the moment
the purfuit was given up.

After we had continued to chafe for an hour,
we difcovered at a diftance a number of fhips,
bearing Englifh colours, as was thought; our
people began to make fure of victory, as the fhips
could not fail of being intercepted.   Their
fpirits revived, till they heard a falute of twenty-
two guns, which was returned by the Spanifh
Admiral.   This fleet, which they had taken to
be the Englifh, and which had been already furrounded, confifted of fix Dutch merchantmen,
convoyed by a fingle frigate; and were fuffered
to proceed on their courfe, at the expence of a
falute.   Every report of the guns was a death-
blow to our expectations, and gave another inftance of our blunders.   The whole fleet flacken-
ed fail, was ordered to move in three divifions,
and fteered to the Weft North Weft.

From the moment that the fleet left fight of
Plymouth, and that all hopes of taking this fort were
loft, I was quite out of fpirits and difgufted; and
finding that I was now of no ufe on board, and
that my health was impaired, I requefted leave
of the Admiral to let me take the opportunity
of returning home in the Triton, which was going
back

back to France. He confented, and accordingly I left the Bretagne on the 3d of September, at fix o'clock in the evening; and the next day at noon, we anchored in the harbour of Breft.

I only ftopped three days at Breft, to let Count d'Orvilliers' meffenger get the ftart of me in acquainting the Minifter with the particulars of our proceedings, as I had been requefted. Probably he was afraid that my report would not be in his favour; but from all I have faid, it will eafily be feen what opinion I had formed of this general-officer. Both to the Minifters, and to every body elfe before whom I have fpoken of him, I have held the fame language as in thefe memoirs. Count d'Orvilliers, to the qualifications of a good Admiral, united a degree of weaknefs, which is often obferved in great men. As he had too much diffidence in his abilities, he never maintained with fufficient firmnefs, his own opinion, though it was the beft; nor enforced his firft orders, though they were always judicious; he was too eafily perfuaded that he was miftaken.

The day I landed, I fupped at M. De la Porte's, with whom I had a good deal of converfation about the fleet; but I took care to make no remarks upon Count d'Orvilliers, which could tend

to

to call in queſtion his abilities, or raiſe any doubts about the propriety of his meaſures.

I ſpent the whole of the next day with the ſame perſon, excepting a viſit which I made in the afternoon to ſome ladies, in whoſe company I met with ſeveral officers of the marine. In the courſe of our converſation, I was aſked what ſort of accommodation I had found on ſhip board: I replied, that my attendants had ſuffered a good deal *; and that as for myſelf, I expected to have been better off, after what Count d'Orvilliers, and the Miniſter had told me: I added, that this was entirely owing to my being prevented, by

* I had expected that my ſervants, or at leaſt my couriers, would have been ſuffered to eat of what came from the officers' table; but they were all of them put upon ſailors' allowance; and as they were not accuſtomed to live upon cheeſe and ſalt fiſh, they were nearly ſtarved. I complained of this, and was anſwered, that what came from the officers' table, was but juſt enough for their own ſervants. This ſeemed to be a ſatisfactory anſwer: but I was ſoon afterwards informed, that they made a trade of theſe leavings of the tables, and that a good meal might be had upon paying for it: yet, in ſpite of this monopoly, I contrived that my people ſhould get a comfortable nouriſhment.

The poor ſailors and convaleſcents, who required ſome little niceties to create an appetite, were obliged, when they were out of money, to ſell their allowance of proviſions to the cook, and amongſt one another, to procure in this way, at a very dear rate, a mouthful of freſh meat.

circum-

circumstances, from getting on board till after all the births had been occupied: but I observed, that I had no complaints to make against the officers on this head; nor was I over difficult, for I had undergone many hardships and difficulties at sea, for nearly two years before; but nevertheless I expected to have been better off on board the Admiral's ship. Some of the common volunteers had better births than I had*.

On the 6th I paid a visit to the Marquis d'Aubeterre, and to M. de Langeron; but did not enter into any particular conversation respecting the fleet. On the 7th I left Brest, in company with Captain Hamilton, who was irritated against Count d'Orvilliers, for the severe reprimand which he had received from him on the 31st of August. He sought to be revenged in a cruel manner, by spreading abroad unfavourable reports of him, and by accusing him as the cause of the

---

* The day I set out from Versailles, M. de Sartine told me, that he had received a letter from Count d'Orvilliers, in which he mentioned, that they had fitted out a small apartment for me in the council-chamber; where he assured me, I should be comfortably off. An apartment had, indeed, been fitted out for me, but had been pulled to pieces again, before I got on board.

I 3 bad

bad fuccefs of the expedition. I remonftrated
with him on this point; but he felt himfelf fo
much hurt, that it was without effect.

In the mean time, the importance of my meafures, and the ardour and intrepidity which I fhewed, had drawn upon me the attention of the
public, and excited envy. I paffed for being the
perfon who had faid all that this officer had
uttered; becaufe it was not known that he was
come on fhore, but it was well known that I was.
He went on before me, and continued to propa-
gate the fame reports againft the Admiral and
the fleet. All this was laid to my charge. I did
not hear of thefe reports till two months afterwards, and I only mention them here to excul-
pate myfelf from being the author of them;
and to fhew that I did not deferve the fevere
reproaches, which were caft upon me on this account.

I was very near being killed about forty leagues
from Breft, owing to the careleffnefs of the
poftillions; but luckily my carriage happened to
be the only fufferer. I did not come off fo well
in going into Rennes; for one of the wheels
being caught in the fpring, I ordered the driver

to

to ftop, that I might examine it: whilft I was
imprudently trying to difengage it, he, for want
of attending to what I was about, drove on;
and, as I had not time to draw my arm away,
it muft have been inevitably torn to pieces, if
the axle-tree had not broken; by which accident
the wheel was let loofe but my right hand was
badly crufhed by the overturning of the carriage.
It happened at midnight. I was immediately
carried to the neareft inn, for the neceffary affiftance. The Intendant of the province having
heard of my accident; came at eight o'clock in
the morning, to offer me his fervices; I thought
myfelf much indebted, for this attention, to a
magiftrate who had no acquaintance with me.
He brought me an invitation to dine with the
Bifhop of Rennes; but I thought I could not
accept it, on account of my accident, and therefore only promifed to make him a call. This
Prelate received me with particular civility; he
talked to me a good deal about my own affairs,
and told me, that being intimately acquainted with
M. de Sartine, he knew all my tranfactions. I
attributed this kind reception to the favourable
opinion, which the Minifter had given him of
me. He, moreover, told me, that he received
twice a week an exact journal of the proceedings
of the fleet; and, indeed, he appeared to me to be

very

very well informed *. I talked to him without
referve of the faults which had been committed;
and we joined in lamenting the little advantage
that had been derived from an expedition, which
had raifed fuch great expectations. He preffed
me fo ftrongly to dine with him, that notwithftanding my wounded hand, I thought I could not
in politenefs refufe him. Befides other company,
there were two colonels of the Infantry, who pre-

* This puts me in mind of an abufe, which I fhould. not otherwife have mentioned. Whenever a frigate was difpatched from
the fleet, every body had the liberty of fending letters by it;
this gave the enemy an opportunity of coming at the knowledge
of every thing that paffed on board. For whilft the fleet was
employed upon the Spanifh coaft, in fettling their line of battle,
and in repeating the fignals; drawings and defcriptions of the
whole, were received in England, even before the plan of them
had been diftributed on board each fhip; the Avignon-Gazette
made mention of this; at which they were furprifed, though
it was plain enough how it happened; fince the perfons who
had the management of thefe operations of the fleet, fold for
24 fous a fheet, every thing that was printed on board. One
of the failors bought for me a book containing a compleat and
coloured collection of all the fignals, and likewife an account of
all the orders of the fleet, for which he gave a louis-dor; fimilar
copies were fent on fhore: if the parcels were too big to be put in
the letter-bag, they were given to the boat's crews of the frigates,
with directions to deliver them to fuch and fuch perfons at Breft.
By the fame means that every failor was acquainted with the actual
ftate of the fleet, and what ftock of provifions there was on board;
not only France, but England, got intelligence of it.

tended

tended to know the particulars refpecting the tranfactions in which I had been engaged, and related many circumftances, that I knew nothing about, and to which I replied only by a fmile, which they took for a mark of approbation. Thefe abfurdities, which I did not then take the trouble to contradict, were afterwards laid to my charge at Paris.

I fet out from Rennes at midnight. On the 11th I arrived at Alençon, where my hand giving me much pain, I ftopped fome hours to get it dreffed, and alfo to repair my carriage, which had been again broken. Here I received a vifit from Mr. Boteler, Captain of the Ardent; to whom, as he was out of money, I offered my purfe. He took 200 pounds fterling upon his word of honour; and remitted me the money immediately after his return to London. I had, at different times, affifted in this way above 60 perfons, as well officers as merchants, whilft they were prifoners in England, to enable them to return to their country; and, I may add, to the honour of all thofe whom I had thus relieved, that they took care to reimburfe me, on their return to France.

On

On the 12th, at nine o'clock in the evening, I arrived at Verſailles. The day after, I had a ſhort interview with M. de Sartine, whom I found very much grieved at the bad news he had received from Count d Orvilliers, and at what he had collected from Mr. Hamilton, who had waited upon him three days before me. I could not ſtay to enter into particulars with him, my hand being ſo much inflamed as to threaten a mortification, which obliged me to go to Paris, where I arrived at noon, and went to bed.

I was here confined to my bed for about a month, and was in danger of loſing my hand. When I was able to ſit up, I heard that many falſe reports had been maliciouſly ſpread againſt me, and that my enemies had even gone ſo far as to accuſe me of treachery towards government. As ſoon as I was able to go out, I went to M. de Sartine, and expreſſed my uneaſineſs on this head. He was ſo good as to tell me that I might reſt perfectly eaſy reſpecting the Miniſtry's opinion with regard to myſelf. From that moment, therefore, I paid no ſort of attention to theſe public reports, being perſuaded that they would ceaſe of themſelves, as they had no other foundation but the malevolent diſpoſition of ſome perſons who were jealous of my advancement.

In

In the mean time, I ftill continued to receive difpatches from England. Thofe of my people there, who had expected to make large fortunes, were quite vexed at the bad fuccefs of our proceedings; but though they thought they had been hitherto by no means rewarded in proportion to their trouble, yet they were not without hopes. They informed me, that notwithftanding the late alarm, Plymouth was not yet put into a proper ftate of defence; that they were the more inattentive in this refpect, from concluding that France had no defign againft it; fince the combined fleet had neglected to take poffeffion of it; that they had, therefore, fent only one battalion of militia, which was quartered in the town, without reinforcing the fort; fo that the enterprife was ftill as practicable as ever. As all my agents therefore ftill remained faithful to me, I thought the project fhould not yet be given up; and as foon as I was fufficiently recovered from my illnefs, I fuperintended the execution of an accurate model of this fort, in white ftone.

I drew up a plan of attack, together with particular directions refpecting the preparations. I reduced the troops that were to be embarked to 2000, and the number of thofe who were to be employed in taking the fort, to 400. I required one fhip of the line, one frigate, and two tranfports;

ports; by means of which Plymouth might
have been taken, before they had the leaft fufpicion of our defign. As the nights were getting
longer, it was a favourable time for the undertaking. There were ftill fome land-forces, on
the fea coaft, and our fleet had put into harbour
for the feafon; fo that we had no preparations
to make which could excite fufpicions in England,
where the largeft fhips of the line had gone
into dock for the winter; a circumftance which
rendered the enterprife ftill more important, fince
by taking Plymouth, we fhould, at the fame time,
get poffeffion of thefe fhips. I laid before M. de
Sartine the above mentioned plan; who, after
having examined it, thought it a good one, and
began to entertain new hopes. He mentioned it
to Count de Maurepas, who feemed defirous
of being made acquainted with it. Accordingly
I waited upon him, and he examined very atten-
tively my model and papers. He ftarted feveral
difficulties, which I eafily removed. He then
appeared to be quite fatisfied, and ordered me to
lay the whole before the Minifter for the war
department; adding, that the fame fhould be afterwards taken into confideration before the
board of Minifters. Prince de Montbarey, having in the like manner examined my model and
plan of attack, told me, that it would be neceffary

to

to fend for M. de B———, to confult with him upon the fubject. I afterwards fhewed them to
Count de Vergennes, who feemed to approve
of them. When this matter was difcuffed before
the board of Minifters, objections were made, as
to the probability of fuccefs; which not being
fatisfactorily anfwered, the bufinefs was turned over
from one meeting to another, without coming to
any determination; fo that at the end of Decem-
ber, it was not yet refolved what meafure fhould
be taken.

M. de Sartine gave me exprefs orders to keep
matters going on with the fame activity. I then
obferved to him, that I had no more money of my
own left, having fpent it all in the fervice of government, as he had defired. I therefore requefted him to reimburfe me; he then afked me
for a particular ftatement of my expences, to lay
before the King; which I accordingly drew up, in
the following form,

*General ftatement of expences incurred on the King's
account, and of the fums due to me on the 1ft of January, 1780.*

French livres.

Due to me, on the 1ft of July 1779, for
   money which I had then advanced,
   viz. 4863l. 10s. fterling, or —   116,724
Current

Current expences at the monthly rate of
37,368 livres, at which they had been
fixed by M. de Sartine, in June 1778;
for 6 months, from the 1ft of July
1779, to the 1ft of January 1780,
viz. 9342l. fterling, or   ———   224,208

Additions to the falaries of 640l. fterling per month, agreed upon, on re-
newing the engagements, and amount-
ing for 6 months to 3,840l. fterling, or 92,160

Extraordinary expences on account of
the pilots, viz. 3000l. fterling, or   72,000

Pofting, and wages of the meffengers from
Calais to Verfailles, for 6 months, viz.
83l. 6s. 8d. fterling, or   —   —   2,000
                         ————————

Sum total of money advanced to the 1ft
of January 1780, viz. 21,128l. 16s.
8d. fterling, or — — — 507,092

The minifter received this account, with a promife
to examine it. In the mean while, as they had not
come to any refolution refpecting Plymouth, I was
put off from day to day. M. de B—— was con-
fulted, but this did not ferve to forward the bufinefs. All this time I had kept my agents in expectation that the enterprife would be foon undertaken, and they accordingly redoubled their zeal
and exertions. At length, when I thought govern-

4   ment

ment would determine upon executing my plan, M.
de Sartine told me, that they had refolved to give
it up. This was a thunder-ftroke to me, for I had
ventured all my fortune on this undertaking, and
even much more, if I fhould be obliged to fulfil all
my written agreements. Notwithftanding I was,
in fact, pennylefs, the minifter, ever fince I had
given in my ftatement of expences, had ftill kept
putting me off, faying, that it was impoffible for
him, under the prefent circumftances, to pay fuch
a large fum; this delay reduced me to the greateft
difficulties.

In confequence of the minifter's refufing to make
ufe of the meafures which I propofed, I thought I would
apply to the Court of Spain, by means of their am-
baffador. I therefore wrote to Count d'Arranda,
requefting him to appoint an hour when I might
fee him alone, as I had an affair of confequence to
fpeak to him upon. He accordingly appointed an hour,
and I waited upon him. Without fuffering me to explain myfelf, he immediately told me that he knew
I was come to fpeak to him concerning a plan for
taking Plymouth, which he had been already informed of at M. de Maurepas'. I anfwered, that he
had indeed gueffed right; we then entered into particulars (he had not heard of the refolution which
the board of minifters had come to) and after he
had obtained full information on the fubject, he
told

told me, that he would undertake to prevail upon the Court of Madrid to furnifh me with the fhips I required, and 1000 men, provided France would give the other 1000. He promifed to make this propofal to the minifters two days afterwards. I begged him, however, not to mention that he had feen me, or that I had fpoken to him at all upon the fubject. He appointed a time when I fhould wait upon him, after his return from Verfailles. I waited upon M. de Sartine the fame day, and requefted him to allow me to propofe the Plymouth affair to Spain; he told me he would fpeak about it, and then give me an anfwer. The next day he informed me, that I was exprefsly forbid to make any fuch propofal. I found myfelf a good deal embarraffed, for I had already done fo; I had not an opportunity of feeing Count d'Arranda to warn him of this; but he, neverthelefs, took care not to expofe me; for, when he went to M. de Maurepas', and was afked what I had been doing at his houfe, fuch a day, at fuch an hour? he replied, that I had come to him about fome affairs of mine in Spain, and that he had fpoken to me concerning a plan for taking Plymouth, of which he had had fome information about a fortnight before, and that we had talked pretty fully upon the fubject; he added, that as far as he was able to judge, it was a very promifing enterprize. This was all the converfation they had

respecting

respecting this matter. On his return to Paris, he sent for me, and informed me of the particulars which I have just mentioned. I perceived from hence that they watched my proceedings; and after the injunction which had been laid upon me, I gave up the scheme of engaging Spain to join in this cause.

I informed my agents of the bad success which I had met with, that I might not keep them any longer in a state of suspense; this intelligence caused them much uneasiness. I was too much vexed at the thoughts of such an expedition not taking place, to neglect any attempt to prevail upon the ministers to adopt my project. I consulted my agents and friends, and we agreed to try the measure at our own risks; we considered how much money we could raise in England on our joint credit, and we found that it amounted to about four millions of French livres, taking into the account what was due to me from the king, together with 250,000 livres of my own lent out upon bonds, and the property of my agents. When I found I was certain of this sum of money, I made an offer to the minister, of paying to the king three millions of livres in ready money, provided I should be furnished with a 64 man of war, a frigate, two transports, and 2000 land forces.

K   Four

Four days were taken to examine my propofal, at the end of which it was rejected.

My terms were by no means difficult; I engaged to deliver up the fort to the king, after I had taken poffeffion of it, upon having the money which I was to advance, returned to me; and as for the reft I trufted to his Majefty's bounty. But it was held out that it did not become his Majefty to accept of fuch offers. I cannot help thinking however, that it would be difficult to produce a greater inftance of *difintereftednefs* and *patriotifm.* I had been exprefsly forbid from communicating to any body, any particulars refpecting the bufinefs in which I had been employed. I had attended to this injunction with great exactnefs, fo much fo as not to confult with any perfon, how I fhould proceed on the prefent difficult occafion.

In the mean while, M. de Sartine ordered me to put my papers into Count d'Eftaing's hands. I therefore waited upon him feveral times at Paffy: I informed him of my embarraffment in confequence of the money I had advanced; and talked to him about my intention of laying before the King, a particular account of my whole proceedings. He reprefented to me that the minifters might perhaps be

offended

offended at such a step, and that I should first of all try some other method of getting back the money. Accordingly I applied to Count de Maurepas, who told me that it was M. de Sartine's business to settle this matter, and that he had spoken to him about it. I moreover wrote to Count de Vergennes, who was so good as to apply by letter to M. de Sartine in my behalf; but, whether it was from inattention or design, he sent my letter along with his. This letter of mine might perhaps contain some unguarded expressions; I therefore soon found that M. de Sartine received me with more coolness, without however destroying my expectations of being repaid. He told me that I was accused of living in a very expensive style at Paris, and of not being sufficiently guarded in my conversation. I felt these reproaches the more sensibly, as they were without foundation, for I lived quite retired, and never went out to make visits; I told him so, and added, that I would defy any body to prove before him, that I had ever been heard to talk about the affairs of government. As he did not appear to be quite satisfied, I took the liberty of writing to him, expressing how much I was grieved at finding he had altered his opinion of me, and withdrawn his confidence. This letter produced a good effect, and I had the satisfaction to see that he began to treat me again with his former kindness.

When

When I found they had given up every idea of invading England, I defired four of my agents, upon whom I could depend, to enter themfelves in the troops which were embarking for Gibraltar, and the ifland of Minorca. Before they fet out, I put into their hands fome written directions refpecting what they were to do when I came there. Some time after their departure, M. de Sartine ordered me to cruife off Ufhant, in one of my fhips, for the purpofe of watching one of the enemy's fquadrons, which meant to intercept the French veffels in which M. de Rochambeau's army was to be fent to America, and to favour the failing of thefe tranfports from Breft, by bringing them immediate intelligence of what I might difcover; he, at the fame time, promifed me a fupply of money. In confequence of this, I ordered my captain to get ready for failing, and to take on board provifions for four months, as I intended, after I had left Breft, to go to Gibraltar, and from thence to Minorca.

As this new expedition naturally expofed me to many kinds of danger, I arranged my family-affairs, and making fure of my reimburfement, I entered into an agreement with the Marquis of Vaines, for the purchafe of an eftate, which he wanted to part with, in Alface. I had juft before laid out 150,000 Evres (which were part of the money I had lent out

upon

upon bonds) for the purchafe of the Ifland of Maffaire,
at St. Domingo, from the two Marfhals of Noailles.
The remainder of the money, which I had lent out
upon bonds, viz. 100,000 livres, I had difpofed of
in fupporting the expences of my correfpondence in
England, till I fhould be repaid by government.
Having fettled all thefe matters, and having about
10 days to fpare, before I fet out, I took this opportunity of getting myfelf prefented to the King; I had
ftrong motives for fo doing. I had acquired a hand-
fome fortune, and had neglefted nothing to make myfelf ufeful, and the Minifter had told me feveral times
that his Majefty was pleafed with what I had done, and
intended to make me fome perfonal recompenfe; I
moreover thought, that the honour which I fhould
derive from being thus prefented, might alfo re-
dound to the advantage of government, by infpiring
a greater degree of confidence in the perfons whom
I fhould employ on the King's account. I applied
to Count de Maurepas, who told me with his ufual
kindnefs, that I had better afk the Duke de Fleury
to prefent me. When I had the honour to wait
upon this nobleman, he afked me if I was known to
the minifters, I told him I was; this was on the
Tuefday, he told me he would prefent me on the
Saturday following. When I informed M. de. Sartine of it, he faid he would wait till I had been prefented, before he would give me his orders.

The

The day after I had been prefented, M. de Sartine did me the honour to fay, that the King had fpoken of me and mentioned that I had been prefented, and that his Majefty feemed to be pleafed with my fervices. As I had now nothing more to detain me, I requefted him to give me my final inftructions, but he wifhed to have the King's orders for my departure, as well as for my reimburfement. In expectation of which, I was kept conftantly going backwards and forwards between Verfailles and Paris, for the fpace of ten days afterwards.

In the mean ime the honour of having been prefented to the King, was flattering to my vanity, and gave me new life. Notwithftanding the capricioufnefs of my ftars, and the obfcurity of the firft part of my life, I felt within my breaft a confcioufnefs of my noble extraction*. Full of fuch notions, I wrote one morning to the Duke de Coigny, requefting a moment's interview with him; he fent me word back, that I might come to him immediately, as he was juft going out a hunting. I did not expect, and was not prepared for fuch a fudden interview; I had a very plain coat on, fuch as I always

---

* I fhall produce in a feparate publication the proofs hereof, by means of which I hope to do away all the infinuations that have been thrown out on this fubject.

ufed

uſed to wear in England, and on my journies *,
however, I went to him inſtantly, and begged him to
tell me what were the neceſſary qualifications and
forms to be admitted in the King's carriage. He ſaid,
that it was ſufficient to procure a certificate from M.
Cherin the genealogiſt. I returned him thanks,
and took leave of him; and when I came to Paris, I
went to M. Cherin, who ſaid that he had above 60
genealogies to make out, before he could ſet about
mine. I therefore deferred proſecuting this buſineſs till
I had more leiſure, and, in the mean while, continued
to prepare for my departure, which was prevented
by circumſtances that will be mentioned farther on.

Till now I had experienced no other vexation,
but that of having concerted meaſures to add to
the glory of our arms, which ſome fatality had
rendered uſeleſs. My own private ſpeculations
had for the moſt part, terminated ſucceſsfully, ſo
that my fortune was conſiderably encreaſed; and
although I had laid out the greateſt part of it in
advance on the King's account; yet I did not
look upon it as the leſs ſecure. The favours
which I had received from his majeſty, aug-
mented in my heart the noble ambition, to de-

---

* I ſhould not have mentioned this circumſtance, if ſome of my
enemies had not thought that I had behaved too cavalierly on this
occaſion.

ſerve

ferve them more and more; futurity feemed to
open to me the moft delightful profpects; but I,
was on the eve of the greateft misfortune.

What then was this owing to? My preffing
folicitations, during the feafon of 1779, that the
fleet fhould profit from the arrangements I had
made refpecting Plymouth, and the falutary
counfels I had given, but which had not been
followed, no doubt, ferved to draw upon me the
ill will of thofe who oppofed my meafures. The
rank and fortune to which I had fuddenly rifen,
could not fail to excite envy; and, as I was too
fenfibly convinced by experience, envy takes
every opportunity to deprefs its object; accordingly, my courage was reprefented as temerity, my
tranfactions, as dangerous intrigues, my converfa-
tions as being unguarded, my title as an ufurpation
upon a noble family, to which it was afferted, I
was not at all related; my being prefented to the
King, as a ridiculous piece of vanity; and, laftly,
my fortune, as the reward which I had received
for my treachery.

Young as I ftill was, and having never appeared
at Court, but on account of the bufinefs with
which I was commiffioned, I was ignorant of the

art

art with which calumny is fo active in fpreading
the moft wicked infinuations; but 1 had foon afterwards the misfortune to experience it, in the
following manner.

I continued going frequently to Verfailles, to
folicit orders refpecting my departure; M. de Sartine, though he had been prejudiced againft me,
fhewed no figns of it. It was a piece of policy
neceffarily connected with his office, to conceal
his fentiments. He told me, on the 1ft of April,
1780, that he had fettled matters, fo that I fhould
be paid on the Monday following, which was the
3d inftant, and that I fhould receive, at the fame
time, my final orders. On this day, the 3d of
April, I could not find time to go to Verfailles;
for as I expected that I was on the point of my departure, I employed the whole of the day in fettling my accounts: but I went there the next day,
at 10 o'clock in the morning; and as I entered
the Hotel de la Guerre, fome perfon, in whom
ambition had not extinguifhed every fpark of
humanity, put into my hands, in a myfterious
manner, a letter without any direction. I opened
it as foon as I got into the hall, and read thefe
words, " be upon your guard, get away from
Verfailles immediately, for you are to be arrefted
here to-day." I inftantly went out to feek this
perfon,

perfon, as I fuppofed he had, through miftake, given me what he intended for another, but he was gone. I went in again, and juft fpoke with the Minifter, who told me to come again at 5 o'clock in the afternoon. As I was paffing through the hall to go out, another perfon, who was quite a ftranger to me, took hold of my arm and faid, " You are in danger here." This fecond warning ftruck me more forcibly than the firft ; and, therefore, inftead of going out as I had intended, I went back again into the Minifter's anti-chamber, where there were feveral people, with a view to wait for the fecretary, whom I had left with M. de Sartine, as I thought I fhould be able to dif-cover from his behaviour towards me, whether I was really the perfon intended to be arrefted.

Whilft I was reflecting on thefe warnings, I heard fome body whifper to the perfon that ftood next him ; " look, there are two Exempts in dif-guife, who are come to arreft fome body here." I then looked about me with all that anxiety and attention, which were natural to a perfon in my fituation, and obferved two men who kept their eyes upon me. I went out to fee if they would follow me, but they had not probably received their final orders ; and, therefore, I proceeded without interruption to the *Hotel de Modene,* the

Inn

Inn where I lodged. Here all alone, I appealed
to my own heart, to the zeal and fidelity with
which I had ferved my King, and I fancied myfelf fecure from reprehenfions, becaufe I knew of
nothing with which I could reproach myfelf.
This reflexion, or rather this confcioufnefs, ferved
to diffipate my apprehenfions in a great degree.
At five o'clock, being the time appointed by the
Minifter in the morning, I went to the Hotel
de la Guerre. He had juft gone into his clofet: as
I got to the door, I met with his fecretary, M.
la Croix, who was juft coming out, and to whom I
faid, with my ufual freedom, well, how do matters
go on? very well, faid he, with a fmile; and
putting his hand to his breaft, you are always
here, faid he, but you can not fee the Minifter till
between 7 and 8 o'clock; he bid me tell you fo;
in the mean time, come along with me into my
office, and we'll have a little chat together. No,
faid I, I am going to the play, but I fhall be
here again at the hour appointed.

The air of fincerity which the fecretary fhewed,
would have diffipated my fears, if I had had any remaining; but they were foon afterwards renewed;
for on paffing along the hall, I met with the fame
two men, who had been pointed out as Exempts
in difguife, and whom I had not perceived

as

as I came in. When I had got to the gate of the court, I found one of my people, who was juft come from Paris, and who put into my hands a letter, which I immediately read, and which informed me, that in the morning, juft after I was gone, an Exempt had come to my houfe and had afked to fpeak with me, and that upon being told that I was gone to Verfailles, he went away. I had not walked ten fteps in the ftreet, before a ftranger came up to me, and gave me a letter, adding; " get away as faft as poffible". I had now no longer any doubt that I was going to be arrefted. When I got into the palace, I read this note which contained the fame kind of warning as the former. I felt myfelf determined to face my misfortune, thinking it was beneath me to take advantage of the hints I had received, and to fly from the danger which threatened me *. I went to the play with the determination to return to the Minifter at 8 o'clock, and be arrefted in his own houfe.

But, alas! this ftroke was far from being indifferent to my feelings; for it would feparate me from an only child ftill in her helplefs infancy, and who was the objeft of my tendereft affec-

---

* Thefe warnings feem to have been from the minifter himfelf. *Note of the tranflator.*

tions;

tions ; and when could I again expect to see my
wife, who would arrive in France, in a few days;
and to fhare with her, the cares and anxiety for
our dear infant.

With my mind full of grief, I came out of the
play-houfe, and went to the Hotel de la Guerre, and,
in paffing along the court, I perceived on each fide
of me, fome people who kept clofe to my heels, fo
that by the time I got to M. de Sartine's, I was furrounded by them; however, I reached his clofet
without oppofition. One of his valets de-chambre
told me, I could not fee him; I anfwered in a firm
tone of voice, that I had fomething new and important to fay to the Minifter, and he muft fhow me in.
The fervant had not, perhaps, received orders ftrict
enough to refufe me, when I infifted fo ftrongly;
accordingly he opened the door, and fhewed me in.
M. de Sartine afked me what was the urging bufinefs
I had to fpeak to him upon. Sir, faid I, I am come
to know why you have given orders to have me arrefted. Who told you that I had, faid he, furprized
at this abruptnefs? I am perfectly well informed of
it, I replied. He then confeffed it was true, adding,
that he had been commanded to do fo by the king,
as I had been accufed of treachery to the ftate. In
hearing this accufation, I own I could hardly contain

tain myfelf, but the agitation I was in, was the effect of innocence. The minifter perceived that I
was very far from wifhing to behave difrefpectfully to
him, he was fo good as to defire me to fit down, and
compofe myfelf. He fpoke to me about my birth,
which was fufpected to be different from what I had
given it out to be. I obferved, that if fome of the
parties immediately concerned, or government,
had any thing to fay againft me on this account, it
was a matter which ought to be referred to the courts
of juftice. The Minifter agreed to the propriety of
this remark, and even added, that the matter to be
determined at prefent, was not, who had ferved the
king, but whether the king had been well ferved.
This converfation gave me time to compofe myfelf;
M. de Sartine afked me if I was difpofed to fuffer myfelf to be arrefted without making any refiftance, I anfwered I was, upon which he rang the bell, and then
one of the guards of the *prevoté* came in, and arrefted
me in the king's name. The minifter was kind enough
to fay to me on parting, that he hoped I fhould clear
up my conduct, and have ample juftice done me.

There was a carriage waiting for me at the gate,
which I ftepped into along with three guards. They
drove to my houfe at Paris, where we arrived at two
o'clock in the morning; I found two officers of
the police there, with a great many people; all my
papers

papers were packed up and fealed, and fent with me
to the Baftile, where I entered on the 5th of April, at
about four o'clock in the morning. My people
were arrefted the fame night; both my fecretary,
and my daughter's nurfe, were confined in the Baftile. My little girl, who was but four years old,
was ill, fhe was left in the hands of the guards, who
continued in my houfe for about a month; and I
had afterwards the misfortune to lofe her.

It may be eafily fuppofed, that during this confinement, the ftricteft fcrutiny was made concerning
my conduct. From the treatment which I experienced in this fituation, I had reafon to believe, that
their prejudices againft me had been carried to the
greateft length. I forbear to enter into particulars,
not becaufe I have promifed to be filent refpecting
them, but from a fpirit of moderation. After all,
the refult of their ftrict enquiries, for the fpace of 14
months, has only been, that my innocence proved to
be equal to my fortitude, and that, though I was
treated as a perfon fufpected of treachery to government, I had in my poffeffion, numerous proofs of
having always acted with the greateft fidelity.

On the 15th of May, 1781, at two o clock in
the afternoon, I was at length releafed from the
Baftile; but while the injuries which I had fuffered

fered, were not redreffed, this only ferved to expofe my humiliation. I walked to my own houfe, with a melancholy countenance, and a heavy heart, like one who is apprehenfive of finding new fubjects of grief at home. As foon as I got there, I was informed that my child, whom I loved fo tenderly, had been dead fix days. I found my family affairs in the greateft diforder. During my confinement, my creditors had taken the alarm, and had brought actions at law for the payment of what was owing them. My horfes were, therefore, fold, and all my moveables and plate were pledged, to fatisfy their demands. My wife, who had come to Paris, three months after my confinement, had, during this interval, applied in vain to the Minifter for affiftance. M. de Sartine made fome promifes; but did not continue long enough in office to fulfil them. The Marquis de Caftries fucceeded him, and my wife applied to him for fome money on my ccount. He wrote her a letter, dated the 1ft of February, 1781, in the following terms:

MADAM,

" If you will come to Verfailles on Saturday, between four and five o'clock, I fhall be happy to receive you With regard to the money which

you

you wifh me to advance on your hufband's account, I cannot fupply you with any, till it fhall
be proved to me that the marine department
is in M. de Paradès's debt; and until I fhall,
befides, be acquainted with the fum total of
what is due to him. I find no documents of
this in the offices;. and I think you fhould apply
to M. de Sartine, by whofe orders M. de Paradès
advanced the money which you claim.. As foon
as you fhall put into my hands the neceffary
vouchers, I will do all in my power to redrefs
your grievances. I have the honour to be, &c.

(Signed)   CASTRIES."

Furnifhed with this letter, my wife waited upon
M. de Sartine, who, at the fame time that he
acknowledged the juftice of my claims, told her,
that he was no longer qualified to fettle my accounts, and that he muft have the fanction of the
Minifter in place, before he could do it.

Matters were in this ftate, at the time I was.
releafed; government owed me a very large fum,.
and I had neither money nor credit. In this
critical fituation, honour, as well as neceffity, determined me to take every ftep that was likely
to lead to my reimburfement. When I was put
in the Baftile, the world had feen me in a ftate

L   of

of opulence; but fince I was releafed, they faw me reduced to want. The calumniators who had caufed my imprifonment, now pretended, that I had been obliged to facrifice my fortune, to regain my liberty, and that, confequently, it muft have been difhonourably acquired. For thefe reafons, immediately after my releafe, I waited upon the Marquis de Caftries, to requeft him to authorife M. de Sartine to fettle my accounts.

If I have not hitherto been able to obtain a reimburfement by any means I have had in my power, I can only lay it to the charge of a very active war, which engroffed the Minifter's whole attention, and prevented him from making any ufe of the treafury money, except for the current expences. But the honourable peace which we have now obtained, flatters me that I fhall receive that juftice, which I have reafon to expect from a Prince, who is fo diftinguifhed for this virtue, and from Minifters who are fo well qualified to fulfil his intentions. I therefore earneftly intreat, that government may take the neceffary fteps for fettling my accounts; and left my enemies fhould thwart fuch good intentions, I fhall now endeavour to arm Miniftry againft infinuations that may be made to my prejudice.

Perhaps,

Perhaps, it may be faid, it is not poffible to fettle an account, which is fupported by no vouchers.

To this I reply, that, unfortunately, the nature of my commiffion did not allow me to tranfact matters in writing, nor to fend any account of them to the offices, as fuccefs depended entirely upon fecrecy. But, how can there be any doubt that I really advanced fuch fums. M. de Sartine can atteft what I affert; he had every proof, and fo much was he convinced, that in order to put a ftop to the profecutions commenced againft me, by Meff. Girardot and Haller, bankers, for the fum of 80,000 livres; he promifed to pay them the money, out of what was due to me from the King. M. de Sartine is the only perfon who is acquainted with all my proceedings, which I was obliged to communicate to him by word of mouth. Hence I made more than twenty jour-nies backwards and forwards, from Verfailles to England. He has all along known what falaries I gave, by his orders, to the agents in England: and is not the following note, written in his own hand upon the back of a letter, which I fent him from the Baftile, a moft convincing proof?

" M. de

" M. de Sartine requests M. Lenoir to convey
this letter to M. de Paradès, and to desire him
to explain that part of it which relates to Minorca, *and to tell him also to order the salaries in
England to be stopped from henceforth.*"

It is plain, then, that there were current expences kept up in England on the King's account; and who defrayed them? Why, I did, in
compliance with the Minister's orders, and upon
promise of being reimbursed by the King.

Will it be held out that as government did
not derive any advantage from the money thus
laid out, I ought to lose it?

But were not these expences incurred at the
Minister s desire? Did it depend upon me to
make them turn out more successful? Did not
I carry my zeal to such a pitch, as to become im-
portunate? Ah! I am sure, rather than have
received payment of the money, I should have
been happy to have seen government profit
from the plans which had cost me so much
trouble: the glory of having paved the way to
success, would have been the most valuable re-
compense.

Setting

Setting aſide the money which I claim from the King, will my enemies ſay, that my preſent fortune is greater than it was at the time I was firſt employed upon my commiſſion, and that government is therefore quits with me?

Although the buſineſs on which I was employed, gave me opportunities of making my fortune, yet it was not the immediate cauſe of it. I was ſent to England, in the ſervice of the King; yet I was allowed to make private ſpeculations, which turned out ſuccefsful. I was the ſecret commander of an Engliſh crew, and had nothing to fear from the enemy, as long as my agents continued faithful, and could thus ſafely carry on trade in the midſt of hoſtilities. The Miniſter knew theſe circumſtances at the time; but knew that, while I attended to my own affairs, I did not neglect thoſe of the King. The former were at my own riſk, the latter at that of government. The Miniſter would have diſgraced the dignity of his office, and the majeſty of the prince, if he had made this ſingular propoſal to me, that I ſhould employ in the ſervice of the King, without receiving any return, all the profits I ſhould gain by my own private ſpeculations.

Should

Should it be remarked, that the King has granted me the rank of Colonel, and three pensions, one of 3000 livres, from the marine department, another of 3000 livres from the department for foreign affairs, and a third of 10,000 livres from the war department (in all 666l. 13s. 4d. sterling). I answer, that the above rank and pensions, are undoubtedly very honourable recompenses for my trouble, and that my ambition would have been completely satisfied, if, as I had been promised, they had been accompanied with the cross of St. Louis. But do not let us confound things; what I lay claim to, is not the reward of my trouble and risks, but only the reimbursement of the money I had advanced from my own personal property, on the King's account. The love, the loyalty, and obedience of his subjects, constitute a part of the King's rights; but their fortunes belong to themselves.

I have shewn in what manner I advanced money for his Majesty's service, and I have subjoined a general statement of the sums at the end of these memoirs. I now intreat the Minister to get the whole of it settled. M. de Sartine, I repeat it again, is capable of clearing up my pre-

I   tensions,

tenfions, for I acted conformably to his orders. I earneftly fue for juftice, becaufe it will filence the voice of calumny which has raged fo long againft me, and, at the fame time, enable me to repair the deranged ftate of my fortune. I therefore flatter myfelf that government, now convinced of my innocence, will make me amends for the wrongs it did me, by giving way to injurious fufpicions, and by imprifoning me 14 months in the Baftile. But I fhall wait with the moft humble fubmiffion; and in whatever way government fhall think fit to reimburfe me, whether by life-annuities, or by a grant of land, or in ready money, my whole life fhall be ftill devoted to my King, and my prayers fhall be as fervent as ever for the long continuance of a reign, which promifes *fo much glory, wifdom, benevolence, and profperity* *.

---

* Thefe expreffions are excufable; a perfon to whom, in 1782, above half a million of livres was lawfully due, could only folicit payment *upon his knees.* Our readers will regret that thefe memoirs have not been written in 1789.

General

General recapitulation of expences fixed by the Mi-
nister, and of monies advanced on the King's ac-
account.

French livres.

Expences incurred during the three firft
journies in England, including the
fums of money advanced to the different agents, when the agreements were
made; all which were confented to at
the time, by M. de Sartine, viz.
2708l. 6s. 8d. fterling or   —   65,000
Purchafe of my firft fhip of 14 guns,
viz. 3500l. fterling, or   —   84,000
The current expences, according to the
Minifter's firft calculation, amounted
to 1257l. fterling per month; there
was an addition of 300l. fterling the
following month, which raifed them
to 1557l. fterling, or 37,368 livres;
amounting in the whole at this rate for
13 months, viz. from the 1ft of June
1778, to the 1ft of July, 1779, to
20,241l. fterling, or   —   485,784
Salaries and pofting expences of two meffengers from Calais, to Paris and Breft,
amounting, for the fame fpace of time,
to 279l. 3s. 4d. fterling, or   6700

600l. fterling loft on board my firft fhip,
at the time fhe was wrecked, or   14,400

Purchafe of my fecond fhip, viz. 2,500l.
fterling, or   — — —   60,000

To two horfes killed, and one injured by
the meffengers, viz. 83l. 6s. 8d.
fterling, or   — — —   2,000

Robbery committed upon one of the
meffengers, as he was carrying the
money to pay an agent, viz. 60l.
fterling, or   — — —   1,440

Diftributed amongft my crew at Breft, for
their good behaviour, at the time we
fell in with the French veffels off
Ufhant, 800l. fterling, or   —   19,200

Paid to a pretended ftate-meffenger in
England, 1000l. fterling, or   24,000

Purchafe of the —— a privateer of 14
guns, viz. 1,200l. fterling, or   28,400

Extraordinary expences on M. de
B——'s account, viz. 2000l. fterling,
or   — — —   48,000

All the agreements were renewed for a
year in June 1779, with an addition of
640l. fterling per month, which, inftead of 1557l. fterling, raifed the ex-

pences to 2197l. sterling, amounting
at this rate for a year, to 26,364l. sterling, or   —   —   632,736

Paid to the English pilots, 3000l. sterling, or,   —   —   72,000

The sum total of expences to the first of
July, 1780, would, if the terms of the
agreements had been fulfilled, have
amounted to 64,319l. 3s. 4d. sterling,
or,   —   —   1,543,660

But I must remark that I did not really
pay the current expences, beyond the
first of February, 1780, so that there is
to be deducted from the above sum,
what was unpaid, for the remaining five
months, viz. 10,985l. sterling, or   263,640

(from which, however, is to be deducted
the money which my agents got by sel-
ling my two ships, whilst I was confined in the Bastile, and which they divided
amongst themselves)

The whole, therefore, of the money ac-
tually paid by me, amounts to 53,334l.
3s. 4d. sterling, or   —   1,280,020

And,

French Livres.

And, as the fum total of what I had received from government, amounts on-
ly to 28,850l. fterling, or   —   692,400
———————

There remains due to me, for money advanced, the fum of 24,484l. 3s. 4d.
fterling, or   —   —   587,620

F I N I S.